D0627219

THE
MOON IS
ALWAYS
FULL

THE MOON IS ALWAYS FULL

DAVID HUNTER

RUTLEDGE HILL PRESS
Nashville, Tennessee

For Cheryl, my wife,
who does not read my books
but gives me time to write them

Copyright © 1989 David Hunter

All rights reserved. Written permission must be secured from the
publisher to use or reproduce any part of this book, except for brief
quotations in critical reviews or articles.

Published in Nashville, Tennessee, by Rutledge Hill Press, 513 Third
Avenue South, Nashville, Tennessee 37210

Typography by Bailey Typography, Nashville, Tennessee

ʼLibrary of Congress Cataloging-in-Publication Date

Hunter, David, 1947-
    The moon is always full / David Hunter.
        p.   cm.
    ISBN 1-55853-020-7
    1. Law enforcement—Tennessee—Knoxville—Case studies.
2. Crime and criminals—Tennesssee—Knoxville—Case studies.
3. Hunter, David, 1947-   . 4. Police—Tennessee—Knoxville—
Biography.
I. Title.
HV7914.H85   1989
363.2'092'4—dc19
[B]   89-30544
                                                                        CIP

Printed in the United States of America
1 2 3 4 5 6 7 8 — 95 94 93 92 91 90 89

Contents

Introduction

F ew subjects have been the object of so many books and movies as law enforcement. Most who read the books or watch the movies think they have a pretty good idea of how American police officers live.

As a police officer, I read many popular books on the subject and make a point to see most of the movies. Generally, I am left with an empty feeling when I finish the last chapter or watch the closing credits. The majority of these works are done by people who are not, and have not been, cops. No matter how much the author knows *about* the subject, the author has not been there, and it shows.

There are exceptions, of course. Joseph Wambaugh was a working cop for many years and most certainly understands the subject. I once had a novel rejected because an assistant editor said, "This book is too much like a Wambaugh book in a southern setting." I was flattered, but I do not write like Wambaugh. Finally, it dawned on me. She simply did not believe that police officers behave as I had portrayed them. I knew it would be pointless to tell her that many events were "toned down" in order to be more believable.

Journalists who cover police beats write a lot of police books. Contrary to the Hollywood image, cops usually get along quite well with the reporters who cover them. One of the hazards of being a police reporter is that empathy will set in, causing a loss of objectivity.

No matter how good the relationship, the presence of a reporter affects the behavior of cops; they are not themselves when being watched by anyone outside "the family." Outsiders can come close to understanding, but the only person who gets inside is another cop. Even wearing a badge does not necessarily take a person inside. Those in police administration, training, and other support services are also divorced from the world of the street cop.

I sat down to write about cops as honestly as possible, to portray them as they are, blemishes and all. My goal was to show the world at large the way life is on the street, where real police work happens. I wanted none of the tinsel or ornamentation that often creeps into such works.

My perspective, I believe, is unique. I was not a little boy who dreamed of a career as a cop; I cannot remember a time when I did not want to be a writer. As a matter of fact, I had more than my share of hostility toward the police. Like most of my generation, I viewed police as, at best, a necessary evil.

I am not a policeman who decided to write a book. I am a writer who became a policeman. Cops, for the most part, are action-oriented people, not particularly articulate. They are bright, witty, and good conversationalists, but they are not writers.

This is a book, then, about *real* cops written *by* a real cop. I have used real names, whenever possible, with the knowledge that cops love to see themselves in print, whether they admit it or not. There are limitations, however, inherent to a book of non-fiction.

The names of all people who are not police officers have been changed for the sake of privacy, including former officers. There are also working officers who asked that their true names not be used. I have respected their wishes. Dates, locations, times, sequences, and even frequency of arrests have been altered for the same reason. No person checking police records can identify individuals by dates or by any other means. I have also included a few composite individuals in order to include stories that would have taken too much space to develop separately.

My road to the publication of this book has been a long one. Poetry was my first love, and the romance still abides. I sold my first verse when I was twenty years old to *Mad Magazine*, joining the small fraternity of those who have free-lanced to that publication. Through the years, my verse appeared in such varied publications as *American Legion*, *Cricket*, and *Grit*.

One does not make a lot of money from verse, and so I also wrote Sunday school lessons, greeting card verse, and magazine articles. At the same time I worked at a variety of jobs, including ironworker, welder, truck driver, ambulance attendant, doughnut maker, union organizer, shipping clerk, photographer, insurance agent, pest control salesman, silk-screen cutter, free lance artist, and carpet layer, to name but a few.

Through the years, people have asked me why I never gravitated to journalism. It is hard to explain. I guess you could say I feared that I would like journalism so much that it would kill my desire to write books. I wanted my art divorced from my daily life.

Also, there was the matter of a degree. I was graduating from basic training when my class graduated from high school. Officially, my high school diploma was issued through the Army in 1966. It was not until 1975, however, that I bothered to pick it up. I did it then only because my superiors at the Tennessee Valley Authority called me in and told me that I had not submitted my college transcripts after taking the test that got me my job.

They were aghast when I informed them that I had no degree. Near hysteria struck them when I could not produce a high school diploma. To please them, I picked it up the following week. They certainly could not have a person doing a job on the mere basis of being qualified.

In 1978 I wrote my first novel. I was unable to sell it to a publisher, but I had my first book under my belt. One learns by doing.

In 1979 I fell in love with law enforcement. In police work I found something that had been missing from my life. I also learned that it is possible to love two professions at the same time.

Law enforcement not only supported me comfortably, relatively speaking, it opened floodgates of creativity. At last I had found my voice and my song. Someone needed to speak for those individuals who stand between society and lawlessness. I have endeavored to do that.

Parts of this book will offend some people. So be it. There are things about which we should be offended. Standing too close to the truth can be painful, but there is no other way to learn.

So welcome to a world where the moon is always full, where chaos would reign but for the men and women who carry badges and guns and confront the things that most people do not even want to acknowledge.

These particular stories took place in Knoxville, Tennessee. You can substitute the name of any American city, however. It does not matter.

THE MOON IS ALWAYS FULL

1

The Road to Damascus

Some events affect us so profoundly that we are changed forever. Nothing remains as it was. The Bible provides a vivid example of this in the Apostle Paul, who was one person when he went down on his face and another when he rose blind from the dust. I have had two such experiences. The first happened when I was fourteen; the second came eighteen years later.

Walking from the air-conditioned coolness of the Tennessee Theatre on a sunny afternoon in the early sixties, I was confronted with a picket line of black college students. They carried signs that said, "Jim Crowe Is Dead." It was not the signs that captured my attention, though.

A pretty girl with skin the color of ebony stood directly in front of me. Her path was blocked by two white youths shouting obscenities in her face. She stared straight ahead, ignoring them. A glob of saliva, white against her black skin, was slowly dripping off her forehead, running down her face.

As I stood there, my life changed forever. Until that moment, the word *injustice* was just a word. My innocence died as my conscience was born. Turning, I walked away as rapidly as I could. Before I reached the end of the street,

I was weeping. My two companions followed for a distance, then turned away, shrugging. They had no idea what had happened to me.

I had bus fare in my pocket, but I walked the ten miles to my house as a penance of sorts for my former ignorance. I had seen the signs all my life. I knew there were restrooms for "whites" and "colored." I knew that black people sat in the back of the bus. It is one thing to know, but it is another thing to understand.

The shame has never left me. There are times, still, when the incident comes to my mind and tears well up. That I belong to a race that could spit in the face of fellow creatures was the hardest lesson I ever learned.

I was no better prepared when the second incident happened eighteen years later. It was 1979, and I was looking for a job that would put food on the table and still allow me time to think and write. Answering an ad for security guards, I found what I was seeking. I had been writing and selling light verse since my twentieth birthday, and I had just decided to write a new novel. The long night shifts gave me the solitude I needed.

My assignment was the newly opened Knoxville City–County Building. The security office was right around the corner from the Knox County Sheriff's Department, and I nodded at the officers passing each day. I had no real interest in them. I considered myself an intellectual and thought of them as "hired guns," a carryover from my more radical days.

In addition to my novel, I was selling a few magazine articles. Somewhere along the line, I decided to do an article on bailbondsmen. As with most projects, I wanted firsthand knowledge. I talked a bailbondsman into hiring me part-time, but I needed a gun permit.

In the State of Tennessee there is no such thing as a gun permit for the private sector. Everyone who carries a weapon must be bonded through a law enforcement agency. I went to the then chief deputy and explained my needs. He said he would bond me *if* I would become a Knox County Reserve Officer. I agreed and soon found

14

myself in a blue uniform, qualified to carry a handgun and owing the Sheriff's Department fifteen hours of labor each month. Eight hours of the time had to be in a patrol car.

I still was not interested in being a police officer. For a while I worked for the bonding company as a bounty hunter, discovering that I had an innate talent for tracking down people. All in all, though, bounty hunting was not nearly as interesting as I had expected. People generally were relieved to be found. Running is no fun.

Eventually the bill came due. I asked patrol officer, Sergeant Fred Ludwig, if I could ride with him, and he told me to meet him in the roll call room Friday night. With great reluctance I climbed into a cruiser that night, still totally unaware of what police work involved and with no inkling that my life was about to be transformed.

"Let's go, partner," Fred told me as we went out the front door. "First call of the night. A domestic in progress, weapons involved." I looked at Fred for signs of excitement and saw none. A big, blond man with a mustache and an easy smile, he seemed unconcerned.

"This is a bad one," Ludwig said as we pulled onto the lot of the rundown trailer park. "See how the crowd is bunched up down here at the foot of the hill. Usually you have to shove them out of the way to get in to your call. These people are expecting trouble, and they don't scare easy."

"Officer." The woman was unkempt and stringy haired, as was the child she was carrying on her hip. "Virgil Smith is beatin' his wife and young'un. He's been drunk for two days. A while ago we seen him walkin' up and down the hall with a pistol in his hands. He's threatenin' to kill Sally."

From up on the hill I could hear the man's enraged voice, but I was not quite able to make out the words. From time to time a female voice would cry out in pain. The trailer was pale green; rust ran down the side in rivulets. The entire trailer park had the mark of poverty on it. I would come to know it well through the years.

"Go up to the right. Stay in the dark on the other side of

15

the driveway. Go around to the back of the trailer. Remember, keep low. When you get there, slam your hand on the wall and yell out *police*. I've been here before. He usually bolts out the front door and tries to run. Don't forget he's armed."

My heart was pounding, my breath coming in gasps as I made my way to the back of the trailer. Until that moment, the Smith & Wesson on my hip had seemed little more than an ornament of office. It seemed to weigh twenty pounds as I realized that *I* was the law. There was nobody to call; the situation depended on me and my partner. I felt woefully inadequate, wondering how a man as afraid as I was could be effective.

Under the window, I could hear the man clearly. "Bitch, you and that little bastard of yours soak up everything I make. I could be somethin' if it wasn't for you and her!" There was the distinct sound of an open hand against flesh. This time the scream was from a child. Suddenly my fear changed to rage.

"Police!" I yelled, slamming my fist into the side of the trailer. For a brief moment there was silence, then the trailer began to rock as the man ran down the hallway. He did not run out the front door as planned. The back door flew open, and I had my first look at him.

He was short and skinny. A scraggly beard adorned his face. Long, stringy hair fell to his shoulders. He wore no shirt, and there were tattoos all over his body. Faded denims completed the costume.

"Stop right there. Police officer!" It sounded like someone else's voice coming from me.

The man paused, looked over his shoulder, then turned to flee. Charging in, I struck him in the lower back with my shoulder, knocking him to the ground. As I pounced on him, taking out my cuffs, he began to whimper.

"Don't hurt me. I can't help the way I act. I'm a sick man. I'm an alcoholic." The strutting macho man became pathetic when confronted with an opponent who could fight back.

Fred sprinted around the house, then relaxed when he saw that the situation was under control. A woman about

16

thirty came to the back door. Her faded blue dress was ripped down the front, exposing a bare breast. She did not seem aware of it, however. Her arm was around a little girl of four or five. There was a distinct handprint on the side of the child's face.

"Don't let 'em take me, Honey." My prisoner whined. "Tell 'em everything's all right."

"She's got nothing to do with it, pal," Ludwig said. "You're under arrest for being drunk and disorderly."

"You just go ahead," the man snarled. "This pig knocked me down and brutalized me. I got witnesses now." He half turned. "Go ahead, pig. Hit me again. I'll be out of jail tomorrow!"

I had been staring at the little girl. Every time the man spoke, she flinched. There was pain in her eyes. How many times, I wondered, had he slapped her in the face, calling her a bastard. In the course of a few moments something happened. All my life I had participated in noble causes, but the feeling of frustration that I was really not making any difference had never left me.

As I stood there, emotion rose in my chest. Here was something I *could* do something about. With my own hands—with my own body—I could make a difference. There was nothing historic about the moment. Everyone would forget it in a few days, everyone but me. I would never forget. True, he *would* be out tomorrow. Tonight, though, the little girl and her mother would sleep in peace.

I opened the door of the police cruiser and put the man inside. There was no great light, and I was not hurled to the ground; but revelation had come to me as plainly as to the apostle Paul on the road to Damascus. Nobody else knew what had happened. I knew, though. I knew what I was going to do tomorrow, and maybe for the rest of my life. I was going to be a cop.

As we gassed up at the service center the next morning, the officers looked like different men. I laughed and joked with them as we all unwound from the night's work. They had not changed, but I had. I saw them with new eyes. They were still the same rough, profane individuals they had been the previous night, but I knew then, something they already knew. Cops make a difference. They hold back anarchy. Without men and women willing to put their bodies in the way of evil, evil would quickly win.

I went home and gathered up the documents I would need and, without going to bed, went to the Sheriff's Department and turned in my application. When I went before the Merit Council six months later, they were dubious of me. Thirty-two years old and a history of job changing went against me. Why did I want to be a policeman, especially at my age?

I tried to tell the story of my experience in the trailer park, but it sounded lame. We had no common experiences we could talk about. The people on the Merit Council had not been on the streets. Finally, I told them that the job gave me great "personal satisfaction." It was as close as I could come to the truth without sounding mystical.

The test scores made the difference. Surprisingly, I had one of the top scores in my test group. A few weeks later, having taken a pay cut, I was working as a jailer. It was two years before I was back on the streets, but I never regretted it. I have never looked back.

My first life-changing experience showed me the injustice of the world. My second—eighteen years later—showed me I could do something about it.

2

Combat Zone, Dixie

"Baker 10, disturbance in progress," the dispatcher said. "Man with a gun. The complainant says his next door neighbor is in the front yard, threatening to kill him."

Jotting down the address, I turned on the blue lights and siren and headed toward the disturbance. I had been there more than once. A retired Army sergeant with time on his hands went off on a binge about once a month. However, this was the first time he had brought out a weapon.

"You gonna call in some help?" I had forgotten my partner for the moment. He was a newly sworn member of the Knox County Sheriff's Reserve. A twenty-five-year veteran of the New York City Police Department, he had just immigrated to East Tennessee, seeking a milder climate and lower housing costs. He had found both.

"No need," I answered. "The car in the next zone heard the call. He'll be headed that way if we need him. It's probably nothing anyway."

"Back home there'd be a hundred cars respond to a 'man with a gun' call. You never know what you've got until you get there. I think you should call for some backup." He had spent the first few hours of the shift regaling me with stories of "New York's Finest." He came very close to telling me that he would teach me to be a *real* cop if I could somehow overcome the substandard training I had already received.

"We have nine cars out today. The city has maybe twenty-five. As you can see, if I called everybody over here, we'd still be a few short. Why don't we just check it out?"

"Suit yourself," he said, "but I think it's insane. You're just askin' for a gunfight when you go to do a job without enough people."

A few minutes later I stopped my cruiser two houses from the complainant's residence. Stepping out of the cruiser, I racked a round into my shotgun. My partner checked his weapon and reluctantly followed me. He was a short, stocky man of Italian background. His lower jaw was dark from five o'clock shadow, though he had been cleanshaven a few hours earlier.

The complainant opened his front door as we approached. He was a tall, balding man in bibbed overalls. "He's around in the backyard. I haven't heard him for a few minutes. Better be careful. That looked like a .45 automatic he was carryin'," the man said.

"*Now* are you gonna call for backup?"

"Circle around to the other side of the house," I said, ignoring his suggestion. "I'll go this way. Hold your fire, unless I say different."

Easing to the corner of the frame house, I saw my suspect. He was leaning back against a large tree, eyes closed, clad in Army fatigues.

"Sarge! Put the pistol down on the ground beside you."

He stood up, swaying. "Says who?"

"Says me, Officer Hunter. Put the weapon down before someone gets hurt."

Crouching down, I put the shotgun dead on him. Drunk or not, I did not intend to let him hurt me or anyone else. He could not see me clearly in the gathering dusk.

"Put it down, now!" I yelled. "If you come up with that pistol, you're a dead man."

He took a step toward me, staggering. For a moment it looked as if he was going to point the weapon at me. My finger tightened on the trigger. I relaxed as he fell over in a heap.

"Cover me," I called out to my reserve partner. Running in a crouch, I took cover behind a wall. I could see him clearly from that position. The semi-automatic pistol was lying a few inches from his hand. I could hear him snoring. The booze had caught up with him.

"Come on over," I said, taking Sarge's pistol and stuffing it in my belt. "He's through for the night."

Hoisting him between us, we half walked, half dragged him to the cruiser. He mumbled incoherently as we cuffed him and put him in the back. The complainant had come out on his front porch. He stood and watched us as we worked.

"Do you want to prefer charges?" I asked. "Threatening a person with a gun is aggravated assault. It's a felony."

"Naw, I don't wanna cause him any trouble. His wife died a few months ago, you know. He's a good neighbor when he's sober."

My partner opened his mouth to say something, but I touched him lightly on the arm.

"All right. I'm charging him with being publicly drunk. Do you want to hold this weapon for him? He'll need somebody to bail him out in a few hours."

"Sure," the man said, "thanks for comin' out. I was a little nervous for a while, but he really don't mean no harm."

An hour later, paperwork completed, I came out of the jail office. "Ready to go, partner?"

"You go on without me," the former New York cop said. "The shift's almost over. Besides, I'm turnin' in this shield tomorrow."

"Have I done something to offend you?"

"No, you haven't done anything personally. *All* of you are crazy."

From his point of view, of course, he was right. There was no way he could grasp the southern attitude toward weapons. Weapons are a part of growing up in the South. I had my first shotgun at thirteen. In the South it is a misdemeanor to carry a weapon, if it is illegal at all.

This, in part, is probably why police work is so exceedingly dangerous in the South. Every year, forty percent to fifty-five percent of all officers killed in the United States are killed in the Southeast. It is a statistical fact, attested to by years of FBI studies.

Southerners are no more violent than other people, but weapons are more readily available here than in most places. This, however, is not the only reason for such high officer fatalities in the South. There are cultural forces at work.

Southerners are touchy about their private property. Farmers in East Tennessee tried to stand off the might of the federal government during the 1930s when the Tennessee Valley Authority took their land to build dams. Privacy is sacred in the South.

If you tell a southern judge that "someone got in your face," he will understand it. It is a mitigating circumstance. In Tennessee it is legal to resist an illegal arrest, though not very wise.

By the very nature of his work, a police officer must trample on private property. Though most southerners consider themselves to be law-abiding, they draw the line at strangers taking liberties with what they consider basic rights.

When the subject of really dangerous police work comes up, we think of Detroit, Chicago, or New York City. Certainly, being a cop is not a safe enterprise anywhere in this country. In fact, however, statistically a New York City officer is safer in a ghetto than an officer in a southeastern middle class subdivision. This is not a boast, it is a fact.

I am proud to be a cop in the Southeast. There are stories I want to share and illusions I want to dispel about my tour in Combat Zone, Dixie.

3

She Could Be
Somebody's Mother

Criminals, especially dangerous ones, are always portrayed on television and in the movies as ugly and evil-looking. You can spot them five minutes into the plot. Every cop knows that's not true; you cannot distinguish evil people from anyone else. They do not wear signs, nor do they alert you in advance.

Baker Shift was working the 10 P.M. to 6 A.M. shift. At the Knox County Sheriff's Department there are four shifts on constant rotation—Adam, Baker, Charlie, and David—and each always reflects the philosophy of the captain. I had not been on the streets very long and was assigned to "driving-under-the-influence" (DUI) enforcement.

It is not easy becoming an accepted member of a patrol shift. No matter how well you are liked—no matter what your credentials—until you are "baptized by fire" other officers simply do not trust you to back them up. No one wants to risk finding out that you are prone to hysteria when you are the only help for miles. A rookie gets to "watch the cars" a lot during dangerous situations.

Early in the shift that night, Mike Craig was dispatched on an "insane person with a gun" call. At six feet, four inches and 300 pounds, Craig can handle most situations alone. A shotgun, however, kills both big men and small, so I went to back Craig up, as did the captain, Bill Wilson.

Upon arrival, we found that a woman "with a shotgun" was at the dead end of a small road. I was told to "watch the cars" while Craig and the captain went to check out the situation. Grumbling to myself, I lit a cigarette and waited. Minutes later, the sound of a shotgun being discharged boomed out into the night.

"Shots fired," I yelled into the radio, "get some help started and clear the channel." Switching to car-to-car transmission, I tried to call Craig or Wilson on my hand-held portable. Finally Craig answered.

"Come on up here," he said over the air. "She tried to shoot the captain. He's got powder in his eyes."

Moving away from the well-lit cars, I was blind. "Craig, I can't see a thing," I whispered.

"Come up the road until you get to the grassy field. Turn right, walk about fifty yards, then turn left. I'm beside the house that'll be right in front of you."

I made my way up the road, walked into the grassy field, then turned left on faith. My eyes still had not adjusted to the darkness. "I can't see you, Mike," I whispered into the radio.

"Keep coming," he replied, "I can see you. You're headed right toward me."

Moving ahead, I lifted the radio once more. At that instant a hand grabbed my arm. "Here I am," Craig said, "don't walk into the wall."

"Don't scare me like that!" I hissed. My heart was pounding.

"Sorry, I thought you saw me. Just lean against the house until your vision clears." I did so, bringing my breathing under control.

"The woman's standing on the porch, just inside the alcove at the front door. Look close and you'll see the barrel of the shotgun. I could've got her, but the captain ordered me not to shoot."

Sure enough, I could see the barrel of the shotgun and wisps of white hair, visible on the front porch. The captain was covering the other side of the house. I could see his left shoulder and the top of his head.

"What happened?" I whispered.

"We thought she had run off into the field behind the house. As we walked up, she stepped around and fired pointblank. Wadding and powder hit the captain in the face. I was about to put one through her head as she ran off, but he stopped me."

"You can't get closer to dying than that," I said.

"Mike," the captain's voice came across the radio, "can we rush her?"

"I don't think so, Captain. She'd get one of us."

"Baker 12," Don Hammond's voice crackled over the air, "I'm at the bottom of the road. How do I get there?"

Craig gave him directions, and a few minutes later we were briefing him. We had a stalemate, and we had to break it. "Captain," I whispered into the radio, "if we can get in the house, we might be able to take her from behind. You and Craig can keep her talking."

"All right," the captain said, "but be careful. If she turns on you, you won't be able to get away."

A few minutes later, Hammond and I moved cautiously through the house. We paused at the living room door, just inside the kitchen. There was glass in the front door, and the woman was clearly visible. "She could be somebody's mother," Hammond said.

It was true. She was about sixty—with snowy white hair—wearing a cotton print dress. She looked like a commercial for an all-American mother, except for the shotgun she had clasped in her hands and the profanities she was shouting every time Craig or the captain spoke to her.

"Get ready," Hammond whispered. "I'm going to try and unlatch the door. If she turns and sees me, shoot her. There's no choice. We have no place to go, and she can't miss at this range."

"Do it," I said, drawing my weapon.

"And remember I'm between the two of you."

"Right."

Hammond low-crawled across the room and eased himself into a sitting position. I leveled my sights on the back of the woman's head and waited. At first, it was like pointing my weapon at a paper target. Put one through the brainstem, and death is almost instantaneous.

Then, as if by magic, the paper target vanished and I had my sights fixed on the white head of an old woman. Her shoulders were rising and falling with each breath. A slight squeeze with my trigger finger, and she would breathe no more. Suddenly I saw in my mind what the hollowpoint would do to her head. It would rip out the front of her skull, and the brain would scatter in front of her.

My palms began to sweat. I had read that term many times, but it had never happened to me before. A drop of sweat formed between my shoulder blades and began to trickle down my back. Sweat formed on my forehead and puddled in my eyebrows.

My heart began to run away as another vision flashed in my head. It was a headline—"Deputy Guns down Elderly Woman, *Head shot fatal.*" My breath was hissing in and out so loudly, I was sure Hammond could hear it. Then the most horrifying thought of all occurred to me.

My service revolver was in the shop. Though I had fired the revolver I was carrying at least two hundred times, it had not been "officially" used at the range. I was about to kill an old lady with an unauthorized weapon! It was identical to my service revolver, but it was not *official.*

Internal Affairs would show up. They would take my weapon, check the serial numbers, and report that my weapon was unauthorized. At the least I would be humiliated. I had never even been reprimanded. I shifted slightly as Hammond tinkered with the latch. It sounded like the pounding of a hammer to my sensitive ears.

"Dear God," I fervently prayed to myself, "don't make me kill this white-haired old lady, especially not with this unauthorized weapon." Even as I stood praying, her head turned slightly toward us.

Everyone else ceased to exist. My finger began to close on the trigger. The trembling in my legs stopped. I forgot the sweat drenching me. The entire world narrowed to my front sights as the hammer began to rise. I did not want to kill the woman, but I knew then that I *could*. The lives of my brother officers were at stake.

She turned back and yelled something at the captain. At that moment, Hammond signaled he was ready. Still covering the woman, I moved closer.

"Do it!" Hammond hissed. He jerked open the door, and we slammed into her with our shoulders, knocking her off the porch. The shotgun clattered down the steps, as she fell head over heels. I holstered my weapon and joined the battle in progress. Even with four of us the old woman was not easy to handle. She fought, possessed by the rage of insanity, her strength almost superhuman. The fall had not even winded her.

Finally Craig loaded her—trussed and subdued—and started for the hospital. She was still thrashing around, cursing and vowing revenge. I picked up the shotgun and handed it to one of her relatives who had appeared. "We figured you'd have to kill her," the man said. "You guys took a big chance."

"That's what they pay us for," I said, lighting a cigarette.

"Whatever they pay you, it ain't enough," the man said. "Thanks."

"You both did a good job," the captain said. "A real good job." Captain Wilson is not effusive with praise.

Later, I sat on the lot of a closed grocery store drinking a cup of coffee. I had made a resolution. When the time came for me to leave my DUI assignment, I would try to get on Baker shift. They were tough enough to do whatever was necessary, but compassionate enough to spare an old woman who had tried to kill the captain. It was a satisfying thought.

I had been baptized, and they would not leave me to watch the cars the next time. They knew I could be trusted not to panic under fire. More important, *I* knew it.

I headed in to the service center, reminding myself to pick up my pistol that afternoon.

4

The Moon Is Always Full

Blue light, mixed with red from the ambulance and fire truck and amber from the wrecker, danced across the windshields of the vehicles parked at the accident scene. Multicolored hues flashed across the faces of the officers and rescue personnel.

The officer directing traffic around the accident noticed that the white sports car was not slowing down as it approached the scene.

"Hey you!" He yelled, leaping agilely out of the way. The sports car continued on, crunching through the broken glass and gasoline, a horrible screeching sound coming from beneath it. Cops and rescue workers ran over each other to get out of the way. The car finally came to a halt in the center of the accident scene.

Nothing infuriates a cop quite as much as being ignored while he is directing traffic. To begin with, he hates directing traffic. He hates it because someone will *always* try to run over him, then swear he misunderstood the hand signal.

The door of the sports car opened as the enraged patrolman staked towards it, muttering profanity under his breath. A well-fed man about thirty emerged and stood

29

swaying, his eyes blinking owlishly at the colored lights.

"What seems to be your problem?" the patrolman asked through gritted teeth. "You didn't see me? You didn't think I meant *you* when I was jumping up and down waving my arms? You almost ran over me and about twenty other people!"

"Sorry 'bout that, Officer, but the brakes are 'bout gone on my car. Everything's all right, though. I'm a doctor." He smiled benevolently and staggered a couple of steps before straightening up.

"Like hell, it's all right! Let me see your operator's license."

"Officer," the man leaned forward, "I *demand* to examine the injured parties, right now!" Once more he staggered, this time sending a blast of alcohol-saturated breath into the patrolman's face.

"Oh, so you *demand* it, do you?" A sober man would have caught the tone of the officer's voice. Subtlety, however, escaped the man at that moment. The seriously injured had already been transported.

"Thas' right. I happen to know the medical examiner of this county. Take me to the injured parties," he said smugly, reaching out to balance himself on his car.

"Well, Doctor—if you are a doctor—I happen to know the *sheriff* of this county, and he told me to arrest all the drunk drivers I could find. If you'll stagger over to the back of that cruiser *right there*, I'm going to give you a breath alcohol test."

"I beg your pardon. I *demand* to speak. . . ." A moment later the good doctor was being propelled by the scruff of the neck to my cruiser. He had demanded one time too many.

After being patted down for weapons, he was placed in the back of my cruiser for a breath alcohol test. I had arrived to test one of the drivers involved in the accident, who had refused the test. At the time, I was with the DUI Enforcement Unit.

"I cannot believe I am being subjected to this indignity," he said haughtily. "I happen to be a doctor." He fumbled a card from his wallet that told me he was an emergency room physician at a local hospital.

30

"From where I sit, you look like a *drunk* doctor."

"Thas' ridiculous. I'm a man of medicine. I *know* my limits. I demand a blood test. Your machine's probably not accurate," he said pompously.

"You don't have a choice under Tennessee law, Doctor. But, in your case I'll make an exception. The nearest hospital is the one where you work. I'll let one of your *colleagues* draw the blood. Of course, they won't test it. I'll take the sample to the lab tomorrow."

"No," he said, visibly deflated, seeing that I was not intimidated. "I'll take the test." He was a chubby, soft man with thinning brown hair.

"Hunter, you wouldn't believe the brakes on the car he was drivin'. Nothing' but metal against metal. I'm gonna charge him with reckless drivin' on top of drivin' drunk," the arresting officer said. It was at that point that the first sob escaped the doctor.

"All right, stand here, I'm ready to give him the test."

Suddenly the officer's already strained face took on an expression of disbelief as he looked toward the rear of my car. I heard a horrible screeching of tires, then the grinding of metal. A beat-up old Chevrolet, with a rubbernecking driver had slowed to look at the accident scene. A Cadillac had crashed into the rear of the old Chevrolet.

"I can't believe this," the officer said in an agonized voice. If there is one thing a cop hates worse than working an accident, it is *witnessing* one. It is a sure trip to court. Both sides think your "expert" testimony will help them.

I turned and watched as rescue personnel ran to the vehicles. Fortunately, no one was injured. Both drivers were out of their cars and enraged. An officer went over to calm them down.

"Hunter," the officer beside my car said, looking at the sky, "it's too cloudy to see, but there's gotta be a full moon up there tonight."

Cops fervently believe that people go insane during the full moon, despite statistics to the contrary. In fact the only crime that picks up is burglary, for obvious reasons. With a full moon the thieves have light to work by.

"Maybe," I said, without further comment. I had long before learned the futility of arguing with other cops about things that they passionately believe. "All right, Doctor, blow in this tube as long and hard as you can."

The doctor went well into the intoxicated range. He was almost double the .10 percent presumption level. He wept quietly all the way to jail, all pomposity gone.

I stepped off the elevator into the surrealistic world of the Knox County jail. Though one of the cleanest jails in the country, it smells like a jail. You can scrub floors and walls, but not the air. There is a smorgasbord of odors—food, urine, and disinfectant. Jailers get used to it, but outsiders are assaulted by it.

"What's shakin', Hunter?" One of the jailers asked, patting down the still sobbing doctor.

"Not much," I replied.

"This one yours?"

"I brought him in for someone else. He's charged with driving under the influence and reckless driving."

"It's been wild tonight," the jailer said, placing the doctor at the booking table. "Must be a full moon out there."

"Hey, *you*," a surly voice said.

I turned slowly. It is bad etiquette to address an officer as "Hey, you." The man had a sneer on his face. He was wearing a fleece-lined coat that cost more than I made in a week. His hair was neatly styled and in place, despite the alcoholic flush on his face that told me why he was being booked.

"What?" I asked coldly.

"See when they're gonna get my lawyer. I ain't answerin' no questions until then."

"Unless they've changed their procedure," I told him, "you'll stay here until you *do* give them the information."

"We'll see about that," he said, arrogantly folding his arms across his chest.

"Suits me," I answered. "I can leave any time I want."

"You cops think you're hot stuff, don't you?"

Ignoring his remark, I went on into the jail office to make copies of the reports for the field officer. Arguing with drunks is futile.

"What have you brought?" The booking officer asked.
"Just a drunk doctor."

"I hope he's nicer than the other one out there. Some kind of hotshot salesman. Says he can buy and sell everyone down here. We don't even know his name yet."

"Got a fighter in the bay," the sergeant said from the desk, "Send two jailers upstairs to help out the officer."

On the monitor, I watched a patrolman and his reserve partner struggling with a prisoner as they brought him out of the car. Both of them towered over him, but even with the cuffs on his wrists in front of him they could not hold the little man. A moment later, the two jailers sprinted out. The four of them dragged the prisoner, kicking and snarling, to the elevator and pushed him on. His curses filtered down through the elevator sound system.

"Looks like a man on PCP," the sergeant said.

"I'll give them a hand," I told the sergeant, walking out into the lobby. The door opened and the little man rushed out, head down, dragging the two jailers with him. The man was cursing and screaming incoherently.

"Somebody get leg irons!" one of the jailers yelled.

Bracing myself, I took aim and drove a fist into the man's solar plexus, hard enough to put down a *big* man. Instead, using the jailers for support, he swung both feet up and tried to kick me in the groin. I grabbed his feet and we all went down. More officers piled on top of us.

Onlookers often report, with great indignation, that a prisoner was "roughed up" by five or six officers at the scene of an arrest. In reality, officers know that the more help you have, the less damage you do. Sometimes you can smother a resisting prisoner with bodies.

It was not the case that night. The man had no contact with reality, and pain was not penetrating his conscious mind. He broke loose, leaving the officers no choice in handling him. There would be no easy way. His eyes were wild and rimmed in red. He frothed at the mouth, his stringy hair jerked wildly.

One of the jailers caught him from behind in a choke hold. Two more caught him by the arms. I grabbed a leg, but his body bowed up, dragging us all around. At some point in his struggles, he had smashed his mouth and nose. He was bleeding freely. All the while, he was screaming hoarsely at the top of his voice.

Finally, enough officers piled on to get shackles on his legs and a chain around his arms. We half-carried, half-dragged him down the hall to a room where we held violent prisoners. He left a trail of blood as we went.

Using sheets, we trussed the man up until he could calm down, piling mattresses around him to prevent further injury.

"I don't believe it," one of the jailers exclaimed. "There must be a full moon out there tonight!"

I straightened up my uniform as I walked back through the booking area. "Officer?" A meek voice said.

"What do you want?" I snapped. Being bruised and scraped did not enhance the evening. It was the arrogant man in the fleece-lined jacket. His eyes were wide. He was breathing hard.

"Tell them I'll give them all the information they want. I'm sorry for the way I acted. *Please* tell them I'm ready to cooperate." His horrified eyes went to the blood on the concrete floor. He flinched as I glared at him. I very nearly laughed. He thought he had just witnessed jailers losing their temper. I enjoyed watching his arrogance evaporate.

"They'll get to you when they're ready. I'd suggest you *do* cooperate." I got on the elevator and left, passing the sobbing doctor.

Upstairs, I opened my trunk. Amidst the spare light bulbs, batteries, first-aid kit, flashlights, wires, tools, nuts and bolts, and other cop's paraphernalia, I knew there was a calendar with the lunar cycles on it. My curiosity was piqued.

Flipping through it, I found the date. There was no full moon up there above the clouds. It was a small crescent in the sky. It did not matter, I decided.

For a cop, the moon is always full.

5

Officer, I Feel Like Rip Van Winkle

The doorman pulled my partner Mike Upchurch and my brother Larry aside as they were about to enter a Clinton Highway nightspot. "That guy has a gun. I saw it. He's been drinking and talking about being a wanted man."

"Which guy?" Upchurch drawled.

"The one getting into the old Chevy."

"How about the passenger?" Larry asked.

"He ain't real drunk. Came in for a few minutes, then went back to the car. Watch the driver, though. He's had the gun in his pocket and in the briefcase. I don't know where it is now."

The two of them went back to their cruisers as the suspect pulled away. They fell in behind him and turned on their emergency equipment. Up the highway, I listened as they gave the description and told the dispatcher they were stopping him.

"He's pulling into the Winn-Dixie parking lot," Upchurch said.

I immediately speeded up. Suspects often pull off the road when they are planning to fight it out. Pulling onto the lot, I saw my brother covering the passenger with his weapon as Upchurch yanked the suspect from behind the wheel. A briefcase skittered across the parking lot as Upchurch knocked it from the man's hands. Seeing that I had the passenger covered, my brother helped Upchurch subdue the struggling prisoner. They cuffed him on the back of the old Chevy.

The pistol, an old beat-up .38, was on the front seat of the car. We had no idea why he was fumbling with the briefcase. Drunks do a lot of strange things, though. There is no point in looking for reasons why they do anything.

"Step out of the car, my friend," I told the passenger. "Keep your hands where I can see them."

He stepped from the car, a tall, lanky man with a red headband. He was wearing an army field jacket and blue jeans with colorful patches. Gold "granny" glasses completed the costume. He looked like a flower child, except that he was about forty years old.

"Break out some identification," I told him as Mike and Larry ran a check on the first man.

"What have I gotten myself into, Officer?" the old hippie asked, fumbling through his wallet. He was a little drunk, but coherent.

"Your friend's under arrest for carrying a weapon and driving under the influence. At the moment, I'm investigating you."

"He's not really my friend. He picked me up outside Cincinnati. I thought he was a kindred soul. I didn't see the 'Vietnam Vet' T-shirt until I was in the car. When I left, a guy with a beard and long hair was cool. I guess things have changed," he said with a shrug. "All the rednecks have long hair and beards now."

"Where *have* you been?" I asked.

He looked me directly in the eyes with an owlish stare, as if trying to read my mind, then asked reluctantly. "Were you in the military during the war?"

"Yeah, but I wasn't very good at it. Why?"

"Do you still hold a grudge against draft dodgers?" He asked.

"It's ancient history to me," I answered, "and probably to most people."

"I don't think so, Officer. I've seen all kinds of T-shirts and hats that say 'Vietnam Vet and Proud of It,' especially in these redneck bars."

"That probably means that they never heard a shot fired in anger. People who spend their lives dwelling on a war probably haven't had anything interesting happen since then. People with real pride don't wear it on their chests," I told him. "We've got a lot of professional veterans around."

"Maybe you're right," he said, handing me a passport, a Social Security card, and an ancient and frayed selective service card. "I've been in Sweden since 1966."

"Most people came home after amnesty was declared," I said, curious.

"I was married at the time. My parents had both been killed, and I hardly knew my sister. There didn't seem to be any reason at the time."

"So why now?" I asked.

"I don't know. Maybe I was homesick. I thought I might get to know my sister, but when I called her in Lexington from Cincinnati she didn't even invite me over. I thought I'd hitch around and see a little of the country. I didn't even stop in Lexington. It was obvious she wasn't interested."

"You don't sound like a Kentuckian, or a Swede, either, for that matter."

"I was in Boston, ready to graduate from Harvard when I left. My accent was pretty well gone by that time."

"I was in Boston in 1965," I said with a pang of nostalgia, "or near there, at Fort Devons."

"I was at a demonstration there in late '65. We blocked the main gate," he said.

"I was one of the guys with the bayonets who ran you off," I told him. "It was around October wasn't it?"

"Be damned," he said, brightening. "It's a small world. You ever hang around the Boston Commons?"

"Sure did. There was a coffee shop called The Raven. I

went there a lot. There was a girl with long blond hair who used to sing a lot of Donovan's songs.

"No shit. I used to *date* that girl," he said excitedly. "Man, oh, man, I can't believe it. I come home after all these years, and the only person I can relate to is a cop."

"I wasn't born a cop, you know. Besides, this isn't the same country you left. You'll be a while adjusting."

"I know." He said with a shake of his bearded head, "Officer, I feel like Rip Van Winkle."

He stood quietly as I ran him through the computer for warrants. Records notified me that he was not wanted, either locally or nationally. He seemed to be drinking in the sight of the shopping center.

"Mike, this guy's clean. Do you need to talk to him?"

"Naw," he said in a voice like cold syrup. "We're arresting this desperado, though."

"Get your bag out of the car," I told him.

"Am I going to jail?"

"No, the great computer says you're clean. I'll take you over to the interstate to a truck stop."

"There's been a lot happened here since I left," he said as we pulled away from the parking lot. "I kept up as best I could, but you never quite get the real picture."

"What do you do in Sweden?"

"I'm a mechanic," he said.

"A mechanic? That seems an odd profession for a Harvard man."

"Not really. I stayed on the dole for a while, expecting to come home. Then I started working on cars because I thought it was temporary. Pretty soon I was a mechanic and out of touch with anthropology, which was what I majored in. Besides, believe it or not, I still have trouble with the language. I can speak Swedish like a native, but after all these years I still *think* in English."

I pulled into a truck stop, and we went in. The clerks stared at my companion curiously. I realized that most of them were too young to remember the Vietnam War. Some of them had not been born when the old hippie left. As I ordered coffee for us, I suddenly felt ancient, not yet ready to end my interview with him.

"Is there anything left of the movement?" he asked.

"Which movement?"

"You know," he said lamely, "the things that were going on when I left."

"Do you have to ask? Tom Hayden's married to Jane Fonda, and she makes exercise videos. Eldridge Cleaver's soul isn't on ice anymore. He's an on-fire evangelist. Bob Dylan was a Christian for a while, but now he's a Jewish patriarch. Not long ago, one of my daughters asked me if I knew that Ringo Starr used to be with the Beatles."

"All gone, huh?" he said wistfully.

"Yeah, its all gone." I saw a picture in my mind of young soldiers gathering in a Boston coffee house to hear a blond folk singer. She sang songs about love and truth by a couple of radical kids called Donovan and Bob Dylan to a group of young men who had not yet heard of Agent Orange. It was a group of young soldiers who slept with impressionable college girls on weekends and did not know that a disease called AIDS was incubating in a distant jungle, waiting to change the face of the world.

"Thomas Wolfe was right," he said, "you really can't go home again."

"I don't know," I answered. "I've left several times and come home. I don't plan to leave again. I intend to travel extensively in Knoxville."

"Well, it worked for Thoreau," he said.

"Despite his pretensions at reality and logic, Thoreau was a mystic and a romantic," I answered. "So am I. I think a seed flourishes best where it's planted, and I was planted here." I sipped my coffee from a cracked ceramic mug and watched him.

"You're a strange cop," he said.

"No, I'm not. You just have prejudicial ideas about cops. That's not unusual, though. I was reading Bertrand Russell one time, and cops were the only people that he was prejudiced against. I've worked around the so-called intellectual community, but cops are the brightest and most interesting people I've ever been around. It just happens that most are action people, not particularly articulate. Unfortunately, for the most part, the people who write about us are not real cops. They portray us as idiots."

"You know what I am, man?" he asked, changing the subject as if something had just dawned on him. "I'm a refugee. I've *left* a place where I never belonged to *come back* to a place where I'll never belong." He was a sad picture, an old hippie in colorful garb, an alien in his own country.

"I expected changes. I even *knew* things had changed, but I can't handle it. People with beards and long hair wearing T-shirts that glorify war. Twelve hours in the country, and I have a pistol pointed at me. Now the only person I can relate to is a Tennessee cop who talks like an ex-radical. It's too much, man."

"Give it a try," I told him. "Get back into the university system. The old radicals are still there. They just drive BMWs and teach now. They're there because they never left. They have tenure. The baby boomers have arrived at the seat of power."

"No," he turned up the cup and drank the last of the coffee. "I don't belong here anymore. My roots have withered away. If you'll point me toward the interstate going north, I'm going back to catch a plane out of here."

"Stand on the lot a while," I told him. "Some trucker looking for company will give you a ride."

He picked up his bag, then turned and put out his hand. "Thanks, man. It was good talking to you."

"Good luck," I told him, as he walked away. I stood watching him a few minutes, then finished my coffee and got back into my cruiser.

"Good luck, old hippie."

6

I Always Wanted
to Be a King

When I first became a patrolman, he was a legend in Knox County. As it goes with legends, you either hated or loved him. There was no middle ground. I joined the latter group. He was a man born out of time, and I think he knew it. One hundred years ago he would have cleaned up Tombstone and Dodge City; the public wanted results then, not public relations. A thousand years ago, he would have carried a sword. Warrioring jobs, however, are hard to come by in this plastic and stainless steel society, so he became a cop. Even at that, his time was limited. Modern American warriors must also be diplomats.

John (that's what I'll call him) was a truly big man, in size and in his passion for the job. He was not especially tall—about six feet—but he was massive, built like a short man with a huge chest and legs too short for his torso. When Knox County officers began to wear body armor, his had to be specially made. A shock of straight, black hair topped a round face that could go from benign to enraged in an instant. It was a joy to watch him interrogate a hard-core criminal.

Truly big men share a problem with beautiful women. People assume that when God has been generous with physical attributes, he has also been stingy with intellect. It was not so with John. He had a passion for Latin poetry (which he translated), psychology, and Edgar Allan Poe. It was not something he shared with the world, though. I felt fortunate to have seen that side of him.

Young people today have trivialized the word *awesome*, as young people do with certain words in every generation. *Awesome*, however, is the only word that adequately expresses what comes to mind when I think of John. He ate more, fought harder, and put more criminals in jail than any officer in the department. He was also the strongest man I ever met.

The stories about him were legion. It was not unusual to run into him at the jail on a weekend when he was off duty. He would go out for a pack of cigarettes and arrest two or three people before he got home. I have seen him get out of his cruiser at the jail wearing blue jeans and a ragged T-shirt with three drunks in custody.

One night early in my street career, John and another officer called for a car to meet them at a bar. I pulled up and started in but was met by two men coming out the front door. They went to the side of my car and assumed the position, spread-eagled for a pat-down.

"What are you doing?" I asked.

"The big guy says we're under arrest, and we'd better not run off. He said to get in the first car that pulled in. By God, I could tell he *meant* it."

Other officers boasted of career arrest rates of hundreds. John's ran into the thousands. Bars on Clinton Highway would often close down early when the owners knew John was out. Criminals wanted nothing to do with him.

Sometimes we would stop to drink a cup of coffee, cars nosed in together in the early hours of the morning. Having an extended conversation was hard, though, because he wanted to check every rag-tag car that went by.

"Did you always wanna be a cop?" he asked one night, shaking out an unfiltered Lucky Strike.

"Naw, I just wanted to be a writer. I fell in love with law enforcement by accident. How about you?"

"I always wanted to be a king, a benevolent monarch,"

he said, dragging deeply on his cigarette.

"Well," I replied, "I guess being a king isn't much harder than winning the Nobel Prize for literature."

He chuckled, sitting there in the spotty moonlight. "Hunter, anyone else would be sitting there with his mouth open. That's what I like about you. I didn't at first, you know. But I listen to you on the radio and I know that every time you make a stop, you think this is it, the chase, the fight, the glory! You're not trapped in a humdrum world. You make your own excitement. That's what makes a good cop, you know."

"I think you're right," I said, "the difference. . . ."

"I gotta check this one." He pulled out and left me sitting as he went after an old car with no taillights. We never finished that particular conversation, but I knew what he meant. W.D. Norwood, author of *The Judoka*, said something to the effect that romantics and realists live in the same world, so it only makes sense to live romantically simply because it is more fun.

A patrol officer *is* a king out there on the streets at night. The judicial system is far removed from the reality of the dark streets. The officer may be wrong, may even suffer for his actions. At the moment of contact, though, he is undisputed ruler of the situation—a true monarch, benevolent or otherwise.

Few kings ever received the respect paid John by the people on his beat. It was full of people wanting to feed him, to pay tribute by means of free food and drink. Though he rarely accepted, it was there if he wanted it.

You are pretty close to your dream, my friend, I thought, as he drove away that night. Pretty damned close to benevolent monarchy.

Even kings, however, have their bad moments.

Without conscious thought, patrol officers who work rural beats turn toward an officer out on a traffic stop. There is no such thing as a "routine stop." They all carry the seeds of death. When John was out, though, you paid little attention, other than to note his location. It was almost beyond belief that he would ever encounter a situation he could not handle alone.

One rainy night he had stopped a car at a shopping center. The captain pulled in to back him up, but kept his distance. The driver stepped from the car and waited for John to approach. The captain could see something from his vantage point that John could not see.

"He's got a knife!" The captain yelled. John, however, continued on, as if he had heard nothing.

"He's got a knife!" The captain yelled again, unable to even get off a shot. The big officer was in the line of fire.

As John reached arm's length, he swung his left arm in what appeared to be a casual movement. His hand connected with the would-be assailant's jaw, and he arched into the air, leaving his shoes behind. This sometimes happens when a person is hit by a car. The man's movement was almost surrealistic as he returned to the ground like a bag of rags. The knife, his pocket change, and his wallet rained around him as he hit the pavement.

"I believe this one was gonna try to run," John said. When he struck, even with an open hand, something broke. A man like that seldom needs help, but it happened one night.

"Baker 11, Code 0!" John's voice grunted over the airway. "Code 0" means, officer needs help, now! All over the north side of the county, officers responded instantly. Blue lights and sirens cracked the darkness. If John needed help, something *bad* had happened. I had no doubt of that as I screamed through the darkness, trying to nurse more speed from the Chevrolet cruiser.

A horrible thought struck me. If this person had managed to hurt John, what chance did I, a mere mortal, have? I loosed my .357 in its holster and made sure my shotgun was ready in the rack. The suspect began to assume monstrous proportions in my mind.

At the intersection of Heiskell Road and Emory another cruiser screamed by. I fell in behind him, knowing that we were rapidly approaching the spot. Then, just ahead, John's blue lights came into sight. His cruiser was stopped on the lot of an abandoned service station.

"Someone down in the road," the other officer said over the radio. We jumped from our vehicles, weapons drawn.

44

In the center of the road was John, face down, his hands hooked into the waistband of a pair of blue jeans. The blue jeans were being worn by a young woman who appeared to weigh about ninety pounds. She was on her knees, jeans down around her buttocks, crawling and dragging the 230-pound officer. The knees were torn out of his trousers. His head was down as he clung to her.

"Get her," he grunted as we approached.

The girl was a handful, even for two of us. We cuffed her, kicking and fighting, and loaded her into a cruiser. John rose to his feet and staggered to the back of a car, where he supported himself, gasping. I looked for blood, but saw none.

"Did she stab you?" I asked.

"She kicked me. I was getting her out of the car, and she kicked me. I knew if I hit her something would break. I was afraid I'd kill 'er."

The captain and sergeant arrived. "Where is he?" the captain growled. He meant the suspect, of course. The captain took it personally when someone hurt one of his officers.

"In the car," I said. "She kicked him in the groin."

"That little girl did *that* to *him*?"

"Yes sir. I'm gonna sit in the car. If you need me, yell," I answered. The tension was over. John was in pain, but he would recover. The release of immense tension often causes a person to giggle. I had no intention of having John see me giggling, not with pain in his groin.

Little by little the story emerged. The girl was an inexperienced driver. John stopped her because she was weaving. Her father had taught her something that was ingrained in her memory: *Never get out of your car with a strange man.* Her father had not made any exceptions for getting out for a cop.

So of course, when ordered from the car, she resisted. As John reached in to get her, she scored a field goal in his genitals. It was a tribute to his determination that he was even able to hang on. It was, of course, necessary to charge her—assault and battery, reckless driving, and resisting arrest.

The situation was under control as we pulled away. Then out of the night, over the radio came the voice of another officer who had not been there but had pieced together the action from bits and pieces on the air. All of us knew John was cringing as the other officer called.

"Go ahead," John answered.

"She didn't hurt you, *did she*, John?"

John could not hear the other seventeen officers laughing hysterically in their cruisers, but he knew it was going on. He would have been doing the same thing if another officer had encountered the same embarrassment.

When the case came to court, John was subdued. The case was very quietly worked out. It was explained to the attorney general that it was all a misunderstanding. The officer would be willing to see the warrants retired in return for agreement not to sue. It was very quiet, no testimony in open court.

Then, however, after everything was worked out, the girl and her father stopped in front of John and the captain. John squirmed and did not look at her open, young face.

"Captain," she said quietly, "something should be done about this situation."

"What situation, ma'am?"

"These officers shouldn't be out there by themselves at night. One of them could be seriously hurt. You never know what might happen."

There was a mad dash of officers for the door. Laughing out loud is frowned on in the courtroom, and nobody wanted John to see them laughing at his expense. Every police officer knows the saying, "The good you do dies with you, but screw-ups are forever."

John is no longer with the department. A new sheriff. A disagreement. And he left.

Still, I often think of him on dark lonely nights. As I drink my coffee and remember old times, I almost expect to see him come prowling down a back road and pull in beside me. Just this once I will say it: You were awesome, man, totally awesome.

7

Belles in the Brotherhood

When I first went out on patrol in 1983, only one
woman worked the streets of Knox County as a
patrol officer. According to most veteran officers, that was
one too many.

Some of those officers had seen the first black officers
hit the streets and already had conveniently forgotten that
they had predicted chaos "when blacks try to arrest white
people." By the time women became patrol officers, these
veterans would be quick to tell you, "All cops bleed blue."
They had forgotten their earlier prejudices.

"There are jobs women can do," they would say, "but
patrol is not one of them. Let them work juvenile and traffic control. I don't want a woman backing me up."

Suzzane Fawver, the first Knox County female patrol officer, was a dark-eyed beauty. If she had been masculine
and ugly, it might have been easier. She could not draw
attention away from her femininity, though, even by talking tougher and arresting more people than any other officer on the shift. She was a beauty and could not hide it
under a bullet-proof vest; we thought of her as a southern
belle in a blue suit.

It never occurred to any of us in those early days that we

were *all* individuals and that there were as many differences among us as there were officers. Southern males are
raised to be chivalrous and do not easily change. The gender problem seemed insurmountable—until the world
turned upside down one night.

It was an early morning hour of a humid August night
shift. Adam Detachment was working from 10:00 P.M. to
6:00 A.M. As a DUI Enforcement Officer, I worked the
night shift Tuesday through Saturday. The regular patrol
detachments rotated on a seven-day basis. Nights to afternoons, afternoons to mornings. I had to get used to a different group of officers every seven days.

Passing a small market, I spotted Jack Fine and Jimmy
Leeper. They were having a cup of coffee, shooting the
breeze. Pulling in, I got a cup and joined them. We were
telling war stories and jokes. I have always suspected that
cops in the Soviet Union do the same when no supervisor
is near.

We became alert as Suzzane went out to check a sus-
picious vehicle at a small community park near where we
were standing. Jack went to another channel and asked if
she needed him.

"No rush," she answered, "but head this way. I've got a
couple of *real* dirtbags here." Civilians resent such terms,
but she could not have painted a clearer picture with a
brush and paint. A "dirtbag" is scroungy, nasty, sus-
picious—the opposite of a cop, the potential enemy.

"I'm going that way," Jack said, tossing out his coffee
and heading south. Without speaking, Jimmy and I also
got into our cruisers. A short distance down the road, I
stopped to look at a car that was pulled into the lot of a
closed grocery store. Seeing that it was a *News-Sentinel* car-
rier, I made a note in my log. It was at that moment that
the dispatcher checked on Suzzane, who did not answer.

Failure to answer the first call is not cause for particular
alarm. When a cop is out with a suspect, the gun hand
must be free. At night there will be a flashlight in the
other hand. When Suzzane had not answered by the third
call, we all were concerned.

"Are you all right?" By now the dispatcher was shouting
into the transmitter.

The next moment is frozen in my mind. Suzzane's voice, faltering and stunned, came over the air. She sounded for all the world like a little girl, unable to comprehend what had happened.

"He . . . he shot me," she said.

In the moment it took for her words to sink in, I heard the four-barrel carburetor on Jimmy Leeper's Chevrolet scream out in the silent night air. Then I, too, was hurtling in her direction, unable to think of anything but Suzzane lying on the ground alone in the darkness of that run-down park.

Minutes later, Jack Fine arrived, missing the assailants by scant seconds. He called for an ambulance and broadcast a description of the vehicle. It was an old, white Chevrolet, '65–'67, occupied by two white males.

I would find out later that one of the two suspects in the car had slowly approached Suzzane, ignoring her command to halt. Without warning, he had fired a silver colored revolver. The round went through her body armor and lower abdomen, striking the grips of her weapon as it exited. In momentary shock, she had come to her senses, wondering why she was firing at the retreating vehicle. It was at that point she realized she had been hit.

I was a man obsessed. Officers *know* these things are going to happen. They *expect* these things to happen, but they are never prepared when they do. I was unconcerned that I was looking for an armed suspect. I would have taken him on with bare hands if I could have found him. The rage was throbbing through my head, driving everything else out. Later, when Suzzane was at the hospital and in stable condition, I pulled off the road, rolled up the window, and screamed until I was exhausted. Other officers later admitted to the same experience.

Every vehicle that even remotely resembled a white Chevrolet was stopped that night. A half hour after Suzzane was shot, I spotted an old white Buick going up the driveway to a dairy farm with its lights off. It was a close match, so I called for backup.

Two minutes later, an elderly man walked out of a barn wiping his hands, to find himself facing two pump shotguns. Three other officers had surrounded his car and were searching it. The old man, it turned out, always killed his lights going up the driveway so as not to wake up anyone. On a call several weeks later, I was told by the old man's daughter that he had retired the following week, something his wife had been urging him to do for years.

Hundreds of traffic stops later, we still had not found the vehicle. In fact, we never found it. Someone gunned down a cop and got away with it. It is a sickening thought, but it was not the last time it would happen. The good guys do not always win.

We learned something that night, though—at least those of us flexible enough to learn anything. Women will never join the brotherhood, for the brotherhood, as such, no longer exists. It has expanded into a family, all the richer for the new additions. Women have fought for their place and have earned the right to be out there on the streets.

Suzzane pioneered the way, but she is no longer with us. Being shot involves more than a violation of the body. It is also a violation of the soul. A large percentage of officers never recover from it. It did not help that she was fired on again shortly after returning to active duty.

When Suzzane was gunned down that night in the darkness of a grubby little park in northeast Knox County, the officers working learned it was not a brother officer who had gone down, but a *sister*. Those of us who experienced it would never feel the same. All cops *do* bleed blue—not only black and white, but also male and female.

8

Sugar and Spice

*S*ugar and spice/And everything nice/That's what little girls are made of. So goes the nursery rhyme. As with most myths, it is generally believed. Women, particularly southern women, are perceived as weak and dainty creatures. The concept of the southern belle—sitting on the veranda and fanning herself with a delicate fan—still lingers.

Cops, even those raised in the South, know better.

"Baker 10 and Baker 8," the dispatcher said, "disturbance in progress. Female subject is breaking up the furniture." I jotted down the address, sighing loudly for my own benefit. It was New Year's morning, five minutes after six, only five minutes into the shift. It was much too early, in my opinion, to be answering a disturbance call.

"Baker 16," the second call of the morning came in. "Fight in progress, 25W, in front of the drive-in theater."

"Baker 2," my lieutenant cut in, "send Baker 8 to assist Baker 16. Baker 10 can handle the female subject by himself."

Thanks, Lieutenant, I thought to myself, *what a way to begin New Year's.* Still, it was a reasonable judgment call. A 185-pound officer wearing twenty-five pounds of equipment *should* be able to handle a mere woman.

I drove to the call that morning, moving at a fair speed but not breaking my neck. There is rarely a life-threatening situation at the end of a disturbance call. The streets were deceptively slick; the world seemed encased in ice. Light shimmered around every tree and bush through the coating of crystal around them. People who talk about "mild Tennessee weather" have never lived here.

Turning into the subdivision, I hoped for a quick resolution. In a few minutes Mike Upchurch would be sitting down to a ham and cheese omelet, with home fries on the side and cup after cup of steaming coffee. I sincerely wanted to join him. It was not to be, though.

Ahead in the darkened subdivision, I saw light streaming from the front door of a house. Two men appeared to be fending off a gargantuan woman, who was trying to gain entrance to the house. As I pulled up, she caught one of the men by the arm and jerked him off the porch like a rag doll.

"All right, that's enough!" I yelled.

The woman turned, letting go of the man, who continued his trajectory across the yard and landed in a bush with the tinkle of breaking ice. When the woman turned, I could see that she was hardly more than a girl. Later, when I was booking her, she would admit to weighing 265 pounds. My estimate was closer to 300. She stared at me owlishly through lenses that looked like the bottoms of soft drink bottles.

"Officer, get this bitch away from here," the man on the porch yelled. "She's destroyed my brother's living room. She's crazy!"

"Don't call me names." The woman walked toward him in a menacing manner.

"Both of you, quiet! What's going on here?" I asked the man in the yard. He was untangling himself from the bush.

"Somebody brought her to the house last night, officer. She got drunk and kept tryin' to drag men to the back bedroom. When nobody would go with her, she got pissed. When we asked her to leave, she started breakin' up the furniture."

"Liar!" the woman screamed. "They got me drunk and tried to put their hands on my private parts."

"Who'd wanna touch your private parts?" the man on the porch chimed in.

"If I hear anything else out of either of you, I'll take *both* of you to jail." I was the only person present who knew that my nearest backup was thirty minutes away.

"Now," I continued, "who owns the house?"

"I do," said the man in the bush, "and if you'll just get her away from here, I'll forget the whole thing."

"You don't want to prefer charges?" My heart sang. If I could call the woman a cab, breakfast was still possible.

"Ma'am, this man says if you'll leave, he's willing to forget the damages. I'm going to call you a cab."

"I ain't goin' nowhere 'til Jerome comes and gets me."

"Who is Jerome?" I asked.

"He's the one who brung me here." She sniffed loudly and pushed her glasses up off the bridge of her nose.

"Where does Jerome live?" I asked, my heart sinking.

"I don't know."

"Where did you meet Jerome?"

"At a bar in Grainger County," she replied.

"You didn't know him before?"

"Nope. He bought me some beer and asked did I want to go to a party. We stopped, and I let him do it to me. Then we drove around until Jerome found this house with all the lights."

"*See*, we don't even *know* her," the man on the porch said.

"Jerome is a nice man," she said. "I know he's comin' back. My purse and all my money is in his car. I just cashed my Social Security check yesterday."

"Where do you live?" I asked tiredly.

"In a group home. They usually get my check, but I got it out of the box and snuck out. It was in my pocketbook, *all* my money."

"Ma'am, I'm going to drive you downtown. We'll call the group home and have them come after you. I'm sure they're worried." Breakfast, I knew, would be very late.

"Nope," she said firmly. "I ain't goin' nowhere 'til

Jerome comes back."

"I'm afraid you don't have any choice. You'll never see Jerome *or* your money. Go get in the cruiser."

"Nope, I'm goin' to wait on Jerome," she said firmly.

"Look," my patience was slipping, "you either ride downtown with me, or I'm going to arrest you for public drunkenness. If I do that, you'll be locked up until Monday. You don't want that, do you?"

"I ain't goin' to jail, and I ain't goin' nowhere until Jerome comes."

"That does it," I said. "You're under arrest for public drunkenness." Taking the handcuffs from my pouch, I grasped her by the left arm, preparing to take it behind her. Moments later, I crashed into the same bush where the owner had landed.

I sat unmoving for a few seconds. The bush had broken my fall and I was uninjured physically, but my dignity was wrecked. Never had I been manhandled so effortlessly, not even in martial arts training. I got up, furious, slipping and sliding on the frozen ground.

"Sorry," she said, wiping her nose with the back of her hand, "but I *told* you. I ain't goin' nowhere until Jerome comes."

My baton was in the car. I would never have gotten out of the vehicle to confront a male suspect without it. My chauvinism was about to teach me a lesson. Charging across the slippery yard, I drove my shoulder into her midsection. She staggered a foot or so, recovered and caught me by the collar. Once again I found myself skittering across the icy grass. The homeowner tried to grab her from behind. She flattened him with a resounding backhand.

"Help, help! They're attackin' me," she screamed to the world at large. She turned and, despite her vow to wait on Jerome, ran off down the street. She looked like a small elephant as she gained her stride. I marveled at her surefooted gait as I chased after her, slipping and sliding on the glassy pavement.

A half block down the street I caught her. Jumping, I grabbed her by the hair. She drove an elbow into my gut, winding me, even through the Kevlar body armor. I managed to hang on. It had become a matter of pride. I prayed that nobody would call the dispatcher and report an officer in trouble, not after the lieutenant had assured everyone that I could handle a female.

She turned and tried to pummel me with her massive fists. Hooking my leg behind her, I toppled her to the pavement. As we went down, I drove my elbow into her midsection. It was not the gentlemanly thing to do, but it worked. The wind whistled out and she began to whimper. Before she could recover, I rolled her over and put the cuffs on.

"Bring my cruiser down here," I yelled to the homeowner. I knew I would never get her back up the hill.

"Baker 10, are you Code J?" The dispatcher asked at that moment.

Catching my breath, I waited a moment before answering. I did not want to sound out of breath. "I'm Code J," I answered. "I have one in custody."

At the jail, I charged her only with being publicly drunk. An assault and resisting charge would have meant a trip to court, where the entire story would have come out. I called the group home and found out that she was a member of the sheltered workshop in a nearby county. They agreed to come and pick her up as soon as she was sober. I cleaned up my uniform and hit the streets. Some things you do not tell anyone about, not until much later.

Being manhandled by a woman is nothing new to cops. If you stay on the job long enough, it will happen. The response from fellow officers is always the same. As a Florida sheriff's deputy once told me, "Police all over the world have one thing in common; they are merciless when a good laugh is at stake."

A close friend of mine was thoroughly battered by a petite blond with a purse as he was trying to arrest her for drunk driving. Mind you, we all knew *why* he had taken the beating. It is hard to explain in a courtroom why you punched out a hundred-pound woman. The judge was not there when it happened.

The officer approached the bench, cringing inwardly. The blond stood beside him, sober and subdued. Before the judge could speak, however, a voice came from the officers' section of the courtroom, just loud enough for everyone to hear.

"She doesn't look so *tough* to me."

The officer stood red-faced as the judge called down fifteen snickering cops. All the officer could do was wait until it happened to someone else. *Then* he could have his revenge.

One night I discussed the subject of belligerent females with two friends over coffee. One was a clinical psychologist, the other a martial arts instructor.

"Little girls," the psychologist said, "are not taught that it is wrong to kick a downed opponent. They never absorb the concept of chivalry. That's why women come through a divorce in good condition most of the time, while their husbands end up in therapy."

"There's another reason. Little girls have never been kicked in the testicles. If they had, they wouldn't be so quick to do it," the martial arts instructor said.

"Amen," the psychologist agreed.

Sugar and spice/And everything nice/That's what little girls are made of. It is a lovely thought, but untrue. Women are tough, physically and emotionally. Every street cop knows this.

One officer I know recently came through a messy divorce. He has a new bumper sticker that reads: "You Never Know a Woman until You Meet Her in Court." Or, I might add, until you try to arrest her.

9

The Man with Half a Face

At one point in his dimly remembered past, Horace Johnson decided that nothing could be worse than the pain of living. He placed the business end of a shotgun under his chin and pulled the trigger. It removed his chin, a portion of his mouth and his nose, and destroyed one of his eyes.

The incident apparently made him understand that there *are* things worse than the pain of living, because he never tried it again. What he did was spend the remainder of his life living on a liquid and semi-liquid diet. He also frightened little children, jailers, and unsuspecting rookie cops. Mainly, he stayed drunk whenever he had the money.

When I first met Horace, he was still holding his drinking to a reasonable level, or at least what passed for reasonable in his social circles. Each month he would take his Social Security check and pay his mortgage payment and his light and water bills before he started drinking. Eventually, though, he even stopped doing that.

Horace's face was a nightmare. It was a caricature of a human face, a living Halloween mask. One startling blue eye stared brightly at you. The other, white and scarred, stared into infinity. There were two holes where his nose

57

had been that fluttered when he breathed. His mouth was a limp, lopsided oval set above the space where the flaps of his missing chin disappeared into a scrawny neck that looked like the wattled neck of a turkey gobbler.

I was lucky. It was still daylight the first time I encountered Horace, staggering down a back road rip-roaring drunk. Also, he was not in a mood to resist that day. He *gloried* in frightening rookie cops. He would dance around like a monkey, grunting and vowing to *bite* the officer.

Once Horace had decided to resist, it took a determined rookie to arrest him. We are trained from childhood not to stare at the mutilated and the handicapped, but we are not trained to deal with living horror. Eventually, though, you would get used to Horace. After you had arrested him enough times, the sport would go out of it and he would go along peacefully, especially once he saw you were no longer frightened of him. The first time I arrested him for public drunkenness still stands out in my mind.

"Color of hair, brown," I said as matter of factly as possible. "How tall are you?"

"Fi' ten." It is hard to talk with part of your palate missing.

"Weight?"

"One for'y-fi'."

"Color of eyes?" He did not answer, and I turned to look, a chill going up my spine. He was smiling his twisted, amused smile.

"Go' one weft," he said, staring into my eyes, "is bwue."

"Go have a seat on the bench," I told him. "I have all my information."

He stood, as if turning to go, then—to my horror—leaned down, inches from my face. I could feel his breath.

"Goo', Hun'er. *Real* goo'. Mos' are afrai' to even *wook* a' me." He threw back his head and cackled at my discomfort. The other people on the bench quickly scooted out of his way. It was the first of my many encounters with Horace.

Horace lived in a small rural community where he constantly walked the roads. He lived in a small, run-down trailer and never lacked for company. When you arrested Horace, he was almost always in the company of three friends. They were like a bizarre Four Musketeers. Two were brothers; both of them had serious speech impediments. The third was a petty thief who had long before given up on the big score. Horace never had to drink up his Social Security check alone.

One weekend I was called at home by a frustrated rookie officer. His voice was tinged with hysteria, as if he had just about come to the end of his rope.

"Hunter, I've just arrested four guys out on your beat. One of them has half a face, ungodly looking, and can't talk. Two have speech impediments, and I can't *understand* them. The other one is just too drunk to talk. The one with the half face threatened to *bite* me. Who the hell are they?"

"That will be Horace Johnson, Richard and Robert Keck, and Ollie Weaver. You can get your information from the files," I told him.

"You work a *weird* beat out here, Hunter," he said, hanging up.

Horace was not averse to frightening ordinary citizens when the opportunity arose. Sometimes he would go to a downtown bar and, after tanking up, call a cab. He would stare at the already nervous driver all the way home, then when asked for the money would begin to scream and pretend to have a seizure. Generally the cabbie would forget all about the fare and drive off.

Late one evening the dispatcher sent me to a small market in Horace's neighborhood. When I arrived, I was approached by a nicely dressed citizen driving a new Buick. He was white as a sheet and obviously frightened out of his wits.

"You've got to get a search team out, Officer. There's a man hurt, and some kind of wild animal out there. Call for some help!"

"Calm down, sir, and tell me what happened."

"I was driving down the road, and I saw a man lying in the ditch. I stopped and got out. As I walked up, the man turned and looked at me. It was awful. His face had been

59

ripped off. He started screaming 'Tiger, Tiger, Tiger! Run!' You've got to help him. It sounded like he was *laughing* when I ran off. He's out there dying, and there's some kind of beast out there!"

I looked the man straight in the eye, maintaining a straight face. "Sir, you go on home now. We appreciate the call. I'll find the injured man and get a search party out."

Driving on up the road, I chuckled to myself. Slowing in front of Horace's little trailer, I saw him on the front porch. When he saw me, he began to point and laugh hysterically, slapping his leg. He loved to frighten people.

Early in October one year, I drove by to wave at Horace. When he was not out drinking, he would generally be sitting on the front porch, staring out across the fields. He was there, but the trailer was gone. I got out and walked up.

He stared at me with his cynical expression as I approached. A can of beer was on the porch beside him.

"What happened to your trailer, Horace?" I asked.

"Bank go' it, Hun'ner," he answered, sipping the beer.

"What are you going to do? It's already October."

"Marry a wich woman and move to Fworida, I guess." He chuckled.

"You eating?" I asked.

"Sure. Owwie died," he said, "dwank pain' thinner."

"So I heard. You have anywhere to live, Horace? You try to sleep out in the winter, and you'll end up like Ollie," I said.

"Fworida," he said, twisting his mouth into a semblance of a human smile.

Later, the morning of the first frost, I drove by to check on him. There was a small metal storage shed at the back of the yard where Horace had stored things. Smoke was rising from the battered building. I found Horace heating coffee over a small fire.

"How's it going, Horace?"

"No' ba', Hun'ner. No' ba'," he said, stirring his coffee.

"Got pretty cold last night, didn't it?" I asked.

"Yeah. The Kecks tried to ge' me to move in wi' them.

Can' stan' it, though. They're too stupi' when they're sober."

"Horace, why don't you let me take you to a shelter? They can find you an apartment somewhere."

"No than's. Goin' to Fworida. Maybe today."

"You wouldn't kid me would you, Horace?"

He shook his head and sipped the hot coffee. It ran down his neck. It was the last time I saw him. I went back after the first snow, but there was no sign of him. Shortly thereafter I was transferred to the Beverage Control Unit.

Someone would have mentioned it if Horace had died that winter. I am certain of that. I like to think he made it to Florida. He was a tough old bird. Not many people could survive with half a face. From time to time I think of him. I imagine him in a little shed on a warm sunny beach somewhere—scaring the citizens, the fish, and the occasional rookie cop.

10

The Sins of Sodom,
and Some Besides

At the age of twelve I was still unaware that women had pubic hair. This was not unusual for a southern male of my generation. Our curiosity had to be satisfied with *National Geographic* and secret copies of *Playboy*, which were passed from hand to grubby hand in the preadolescent underground.

The beaming native women in *National Geographic* always had a loin cloth or discreet shadows to cover the area of curiosity. The girls of *Playboy* always lifted a modest knee, almost, but not quite, revealing what we were trying to glimpse. My father considered *National Geographic* pornographic

I grew into adolescence believing that beneath their clothes all women hid golden bodies and cone-shaped breasts. My first glimpse of a *real* breast at thirteen was almost a letdown. My date's pale, pink orbs could not compete with Miss October of 1961. The worst shock came later, however, when I finally talked a female of my age into letting me have a glimpse at the forbidden zone.

A few years later while serving with the U.S. Army, I prowled Baltimore with my friends. By the time I left, I was jaded, or so I thought. Even in Baltimore, though, there were limits. The strippers wore pasties and

G-strings. I had to return to the South to see my first really outrageous strip show.

In 1969 I moved to Charlotte, North Carolina, for no particular reason other than I was restless at the age of twenty-two. I found Charlotte, "The Queen City," in the midst of a cultural change for which it was not prepared. At the time it seemed exciting and harmless.

Topless bars had sprung up all over the city. The bars were followed by topless restaurants, massage parlors, and photographic studios where cameras could be rented, but no film was allowed. The dancers and waitresses, I soon found, wore no pasties at all. I saw Morgana, the world famous stripper, arrested for stripping all the way down to her "birthday suit."

In early 1970 I was working for American Bakeries as a loading dock clerk. A few blocks away was a small cafe that served beer and sandwiches. One night as I sat in the factory break area, I was approached by Jim, an elderly black man who was in my loading crew. He appeared to be almost in shock.

"Hunter, you ain't gonna believe what just happened to me."

"What, Jim? What happened?" Jim tended to be excitable.

"I went up at Chad's to get a sandwich and a beer. The waitress that come to wait on me, she wasn't wearin' nothin' but her drawers. Them titties was starin' me right in the face."

"Did you get your sandwich?"

"No, what I done was got the hell right outta there. Ain't but four tables and six stools. I ain't sittin' that close to a nekkid white girl."

"What if she had been black, Jim?"

"Hell, no. It ain't right for them to be temptin' a man while he's tryin' to eat. Besides, ain't no black girl gonna walk around nekkid."

Jim, of course, was wrong. Black girls took to topless dancing with the same vigor as their white counterparts. Charlotte was in the grip of open nudity. *Life* magazine called Charlotte "Titty City, U.S.A." and proclaimed that only Los Angeles could remotely compare with the wanton behavior in Charlotte. It was a blow for the citizens of Charlotte. The age of innocence had ended in the South.

After the birth of my daughter, I grew bored with working on the loading docks of American Bakeries and moved back to Knoxville to drive an ambulance. I quickly found that my hometown had changed while I was gone. Topless dancers had preceded me. In fact, "topless" was not the correct word. Knoxville's dancers did not bother with the bottoms. They danced totally naked.

There have been attempts to ban nude dancing in Knoxville, but they always seem to bog down along the way. The bars make large profits for their owners and taxes for the county, and there has been great resistance to change. Eventually, however, zoning laws were passed to contain the existing bars, but as of this writing they still are going strong in Knox County.

Being in nude bars on an almost daily basis changes a man's perspective. After several years of being in them, I can walk through without glancing at the dancers. One evening, however, I went with a female officer to arrest a dancer. In the back room the dancer removed her costume to put on her street clothes. I had seen this dancer stark naked dozens of time, but when she got into her panties, I turned away, embarrassed. She had ceased to be a nude dancer and had become an ordinary woman, naked from the waist up. The senses quickly adapt to any situation.

As time passed, I became acquainted with many of the highway's denizens, among them a doorman, or bouncer, at one of the nude bars. Bobby was an ex-biker, with a long flowing beard and pigtail. He took a liking to me and on one occasion pulled an assailant off my back while I was fighting another prisoner. His wife danced at the club, and to him it seemed not only profitable but reasonable.

"What I say, Hunter, is this. I don't care who *looks*. It's a compliment to you when your old lady turns somebody else on. Who'd want a woman that nobody else would look at? Besides, the money's great."

When I went in one night, Bobby was agitated. "You see

65

that blonde, Hunter? The skinny one with a tattoo on her butt."

"Yeah, I see her."

"She wanted me and Teresa to go home with her and her old man. She said we could swap off and sleep with each other and, if I wanted, she could get it on with Teresa."

"No kidding?" I said.

"Yeah, and I'll tell you something, Hunter. That's sick."

"I guess you're right, Bobby." We watched as Bobby's wife made her way across the stage, displaying her crotch to the slobbering bar patrons, naked as the day she was born.

Shortly afterward, I found that Teresa did not share Bobby's views on marital fidelity. I strolled in one night to find that Bobby was off with a toothache. As I stood by the door, she approached and stepped in uncomfortably close. She had just come from the stage, and I felt her bare nipple against my arm.

"Would you like a Coke, Officer?"

"No thanks," I said. It has never been my policy to drink even a Coke in bars I patrol. Other patrons do not *know* it is a Coke, and you never know what might be added to it.

"If you don't want a Coke, how would you like. . . ." She leaned to my ear and named several things that she would be willing to give if I would see her after work. She was graphic.

"Careful," I stammered, trying to pass off her suggestions on a light note, "what you're suggesting is illegal."

"Only if I charge for it, Honey." She turned and walked away with a twitch of white, bare buttocks. I do not believe she had been in sunlight for years. To further the contrast, she always wore dark eye makeup and scarlet lipstick.

In a few minutes I was headed up the highway in a sweat. I was fairly certain that some of the things she had mentioned *are*, in fact, still illegal in the state of Tennessee. I hunted up an old patrolman of my acquaintance and related the story to him.

"I wondered how long it would take and if you'd get through it," he said, lighting a cigarette.

"What are you talking about?" I asked.

"Well, these girls think cops are more powerful than we are. It makes them feel safe to have a cop on the hook. You can bet, though, it would have been the most expensive encounter you ever had. Once they get their hooks in, there's no getting away from them."

"I wouldn't do it anyway, even if I wasn't married."

"Neither would I," he said. "You can find every disease known to man on this highway. Some cops do it, though."

It was a pattern that was repeated many times through the years. Surprisingly enough, though, the girls I turned down did not take offense. In fact, they were among my best informants. "He's straight," they would tell their friends. "He won't take advantage, and if you need help that's not illegal, he'll get it for you."

As time passed and I learned more and more about the trade going on in the flesh shops, my attitude began to change. When I began, my view of "victimless crimes" was almost libertarian. As a Clinton Highway street cop, I came to understand that there are no victimless crimes.

My attitude began to change when I listened to a first-hand story one evening, as one young woman described her recruitment as a nude dancer at age eighteen. The owner of the bar ran an add for "waitresses," promising good money. When the applicants arrived, he singled her out as the prettiest and took her aside to explain that all the positions were filled. He poured her a drink and asked if she would be willing to dance.

The girl—from deep in the surrounding hills—told him that she could not do it. He poured her another drink and asked if she had ever worn a bikini bathing suit. The girl, of course, admitted that she had. A few minutes later, she had been outfitted in a fairly modest bikini and was moving in time to the music, the owner and female manager as her only audience.

Another drink later, the owner stuffed a hundred dollar bill in her bikini bottom. "There's another one just like this when you take it all off."

The suit came off, and the girl was dancing that night. Of course, she had to prime herself with alcohol to do it. After that she was introduced to cocaine, which is another commodity moved in the nude bars, and to other narcotics. In two years she went from eighteen to thirty. When it was over, she moved to streetwalking to pay for her habit. The last photo I saw of her did not look particularly attractive. She was lying in an alley in a nearby city, slashed to death. Her last trick was interested in more than sex.

This pattern is repeated over and over again. There is an inexhaustible supply of young females to be lured into the business. Sometimes I show photographs to friends who moan about "totalitarian states" and "victimless crimes." I show them the photographs of young women with needle tracks on their ankles and inside their thighs.

The old arguments will not hold water. "The girls *voluntarily* do it," these friends say. "There are no victims."

"That's true," I tell them, "but I have disarmed attempted suicides several times. They were attempting to die *voluntarily*. Was I wrong to save them?" If there is a difference, I do not possess the intellect to discern it. A victim is a victim. These users of women—these pimps—who masquerade as legitimate businessmen, kill the spirit and soul, just as if they had put a pistol to a woman's head and pulled the trigger.

A cop learns something that few people ever come to understand. The argument against legislating morality is moot. We have *always* legislated morality. It is one of the functions of government, going back to the Code of Hammurabi and the Ten Commandments. We have to, because if we follow the logic of unrestrained libertarianism, we will have to allow child molesters the right to "pursuit of happiness."

There will always be those who smile and say, "Boys will be boys." Few of those boys, however, get to be twelve years old these days without knowing more than I did at twenty—even in Dixieland.

11

And Mohammed Is
His Prophet

Clinton Highway, the section of Highway 25W that
runs through Knoxville to Clinton, Tennessee, is a
short stretch of only a few miles. Only four or five miles of
it lies within the immediate jurisdiction of the Sheriff's Department. This section of highway is notorious for its bars
and the activities that take place in them.

In the early days it was rife with gambling and bootleg-
gers. After liquor was legalized, nude bars came along to
fill the revenue gap. At one time there were three nude
bars and three ordinary bars in one four-mile stretch. Until the early 1970s, one deputy patrolled the entire north
end of the county. The bar owners pretty much had their
way. The Sheriff's Department expanded in the late '70s,
but little changed.

In 1982 Joe Fowler was elected sheriff of Knox County.
He immediately put out the word: clean up the highways.
Traditionally, bar owners had exerted a lot of influence on
the sheriff's race, but Fowler broke the tradition. He had
no friends among the shady operators, and he wanted
none. The bar owners dug deep in 1986 to defeat him, but
to no avail. Things had changed.

Unfortunately, vice is hard to dig out once it becomes

entrenched. Though only a shadow of its former self, Clinton Highway is still a rough place. It is not the kind of place where you take your wife for a quiet evening. Other factors complicate matters. Under Tennessee law, counties with liquor-by-the-drink can extend drinking hours until three in the morning. When the beer drinkers in bordering Anderson County are run out of the bars at midnight, they come south looking for more action.

Knox County officers are waiting, but the parade seems endless. Mike Upchurch and I made over 1,000 arrests off Clinton Highway in a three-year period, seemingly without making a dent. They come across the county line every night like lemmings on their way to the sea.

Just as vice to suit any taste is available, a variety of ethnic and racial groups is always represented. The University of Tennessee is but a short distance away and sends an array of exchange students up Clinton Highway looking for unrestrained fun. I have arrested Chinese, Japanese, Filipinos, Greeks, Russians, and Arabs. Some nights the atmosphere becomes truly international.

"You know," Mike Upchurch drawled one evening, "we've had everything else on Clinton Highway, it wouldn't surprise me if we turned up some *Shee*-ite terrorists one night."

He was overheard by Darrel Evans, a DUI Enforcement Officer. Now Darrel did not know a lot about Shiites, or any other type of Muslim for that matter, but he knows a good phrase when he hears one. Thereafter, whenever you saw Darrel, he would tell you that he was looking for *Shee*-ite terrorists. Every unsolved crime was attributed to the *shee*-ites. Long after everyone else had forgotten what he was talking about, Darrel went on stalking Shiites.

One evening—about 11:00—I stopped a car that was weaving, northbound on Clinton Highway, in a classic DUI pattern. As I approached, I saw that the driver was a nicely dressed man of thirty or so, dark-skinned, with black hair.

"May I see your license, please?"

"What is the problem, officer?" His speech was precise, a second language.

"You were weaving badly. I need to see your license please."

"I'm sorry, but what is *weaving*?"

"It means you were driving badly. Now, let me see your license, *now*."

He fumbled reluctantly through his wallet, telling me everything I needed to know. A driver's license was one of the things he had overlooked before hitting the night spots. Finally he fished out a plastic card and handed it to me. It was in Arabic and had a picture of him wearing the traditional Saudi Arabian headgear.

"Sorry," I said, "but this won't do. I need a Tennessee driver's license or an international license."

"Is valid," he said. "I have diplomatic immunity."

"Let me explain something," I told him. "First of all, every university student I arrest tells me that he has diplomatic immunity. Secondly, I don't *care* if you have diplomatic immunity. I may not be able to prosecute, but *I* decide who gets arrested. Furthermore, *everyone* I catch drinking and driving goes to jail. Now, do you have a valid license or not?"

"No sir." He dropped his head dejectedly.

"Then step out of the car. You are under arrest for driving without a license and, on the basis of your driving and the odor of alcoholic beverage on your breath, for driving under the influence of an intoxicant."

His eyes took on a wild look. For a moment I thought he was about to become violent. "Not *that*. Please, not that I was drinking alcohol."

"Your grasp of the language has improved. A moment ago you didn't know what *weaving* meant, now you understand *intoxicant*."

"I'm sorry I tried to deceive you, but you *can't* say I was drinking an alcoholic beverage."

"Can and will," I said, patting him down and putting him in my car.

"You don't understand what drinking alcohol means to a Muslim. It could end my career."

"You could have ended someone's life," I told him.

"That's true, Allah help me. A man of thirty years

should know better, but I had heard of these bars where young women take off their clothes. I drank three of the beers while I watched."

"You're trying to say you've only had *three* beers?"

"Yes, I would not lie."

"Why not again? You've already lied to me about diplomatic immunity and the license." He did not reply. It was possible, if he were unused to alcohol, that three beers had affected him strongly. Cops are all skeptical, though.

"Baker 10, I need a wrecker and a breath alcohol unit."

The Saudi answered my questions while we waited on the breath alcohol test unit. He was an engineering student from a good family; his wife and children were still in Saudi Arabia. When the breath alcohol unit pulled in behind me, I walked him back and handed Darrel Evans the Saudi license. He placed it on his clipboard without looking at it.

I was about ten feet away when he exploded. "Hunter, what in the *hail* is this?"

"What's wrong, Darrel?" I asked innocently.

"This thang is nothin' but chicken scratches," he said.

"That's Arabic, Darrel."

"What am I supposed to do with it?" he asked.

"Darrel, I can't please you," I sprung the trap on him. "I bring you your first Shiite, and you're not even happy about it."

"No, No, No! I'm not Shiite. I'm a Sunni!"

"Quiet down back there," Darrel growled. The man became quiet as Darrel prepared the machine for a test. A few minutes later the man had blown a .07 percent, lower than the presumption level in Tennessee. It appeared that he was an inexperienced drinker.

"Step on out of the car, Mister *Shee*-ite," Darrel said. "Go back to this officer's car." The man glared at the stocky, dark-haired Evans but did not argue.

As I was finishing up my paperwork at the jail, the man broached the subject again. "There is a difference between Shiites and Sunnis."

"I know. Shiites don't accept the caliphs as the rightful

heirs to Mohammed's leadership. They believe Mohammed's son-in-law, Ali, was the rightful heir to the leadership."

"And the Sunnis?" He was staring at me in wonder.

"Sunnis, or Sunnites, follow the Sunna, which are the practices of Mohammed as handed down by tradition. There are divisions among the Sunnis, roughly equivalent to Protestant divisions in the Christian church. Sunnis and Shiites are as different as, say, Catholics and Protestants."

"How is it that you know about Muslims?"

"Life is a spiritual journey," I told him, "and I have looked down many roads."

"If you knew this, why did you tell the other officer I was a Shiite?"

"It was a cruel joke, and I apologize. Most Americans are not concerned with the divisions of Islam."

I had all but forgotten the conversation when the case came to court a month later. "Your Honor," I said, "in my opinion this case was a matter of an inexperienced drinker, possibly having his first experience. I would ask that he be placed on probation rather than being jailed."

"Very well, on your recommendation, I'll place him on diversion and dismiss in six months if there are no further problems. You may go," the judge said.

I gathered up my paperwork and went back to my seat. The defendant continued to stand in front of the bench until the judge noticed him. "Sir, did you have something else to share with the court?"

"Yes, Your Honor."

"Please be brief then, as we have a heavy docket," the judge told him.

"I'm not a Shiite, I'm a Sunni," the man said gravely.

The judge stared at him for a moment, then looked at me. I was trying to slide down out of sight. Why had I told him that Americans do not understand Islam?

"Sir," the judge said, "as with so many of Officer Hunter's arrests, I'm sure there is a very interesting story

73

here. However, our time is limited. You may go."

The judge never did ask me about it, and I was glad. Too often we speak when we should remain quiet.

As for the Shiite terrorists, though, I have great confidence that they will one day find their way to Clinton Highway. Every other variety of criminal does. When it happens, Darrel Evans will be ready. He now knows what Arabic script looks like. He has been forewarned. When the night comes, he will be able to handle it.

"Step out, Mister *Shee*-ite," he will say, "you're under arrest for DUI."

12

Come the Dragon Breathing Fire

The first time I saw Mike Keogh was long before I became a cop. I was an ambulance driver delivering a patient to a psychiatric ward at a Knoxville hospital. He strolled into the dayroom where I was waiting for my partner to finish the paperwork. He was about six feet tall, wearing nothing but pajama bottoms, all muscle and sinew. Even when he was pushing forty, Keogh could do one hundred pushups on his knuckles.

It was the first time a man ever made my hair stand on end. Looking into his eyes was like staring into a pit with no bottom. *Evil* is a word used by theologians in this stainless steel and plastic world, not by scientific people. I have never come close to finding any other word to adequately describe Mike Keogh.

He picked up an exercise bike from the dayroom floor and slowly began to twist the tubular steel apart, looking around to be certain he had an audience. A shudder went up my spine as I thought of the strength in those hands.

"Keogh's at it again," an orderly yelled into the phone. "Get us some help up here."

He casually tossed the twisted exercise bike to the floor and walked across the hall to the men's restroom. A moment later there was a crumbling, tearing sound. Keogh opened the door and hurled the toilet bowl into the hallway. Water poured from under the door.

Within five minutes, the time it took reinforcements to arrive, all the plumbing had been ripped from the walls. Keogh stood waiting for the assault. I watched the orderlies fight him. He tossed them around like matchstick men, until finally he collapsed under the sheer weight of so many bodies. Normally quick to enter a fray, I watched. It was as if he were more than human. I remember thinking of dragons.

I was not really surprised when I saw him twelve years later as I did a head count at the Knox County Jail. He had been in and out of psychiatric wards and jails since he was nineteen. At this particular time, he was there for shooting one of his brothers during an argument over which television program to watch. He had sprouted a long beard and had put on fifty pounds since I had seen him last, but the eyes had not changed at all.

Working the night shift—10:00 P.M. to 6:00 A.M.—I only saw the prisoners for an hour in the evening before they were put to bed. A week went by before he finally spoke to me.

"I know you, Hunter," he said as I passed, "and you know me."

"That's not a great feat," I told him, "since I'm wearing a name tag and your name is on the jail list." I started to walk on.

"I ain't talkin' about names, Hunter. I'm talkin' *souls*. Your soul looked at my soul and shuddered the first time you saw me. You ain't afraid of a man alive, Hunter. I can tell that. But my father scares you."

"Is that right?" I was fascinated despite my revulsion. "And who is your father?"

"My father is the lord of the flies."

"Well, if I get your father in here, I'll lock him up too." I walked away. I *was* shuddering, not just my soul, but my body. I had known dozens of prisoners claiming kinship with the devil, but none had ever come close to making me believe, not before Mike Keogh. I dismissed the thought as irrational. The educated mind cannot overcome the childhood training, no matter how valiantly it strives.

Keogh was out in a few months on that charge. His brother refused to prosecute. Six months later he walked off the elevator again. His arm was wrapped in a dirty white rag. At that time it was my job to receive prisoners for booking.

"What happened, Keogh?"

"One of your pig friends arrested me for being drunk." He turned those jade green eyes without bottoms toward me. "I got a bad arm and couldn't fight. He don't know how lucky he is, does he, Hunter?"

"I need to look at your arm. If it's too serious, you may need medical attention," I told him, ignoring his remark.

"I ain't goin' to no hospital, but you can look at my arm." Under the dirty white rag was a sanitary napkin, held on with black electrical tape. There was a deep gash, four inches long. It was puffy and inflamed.

"This should be treated, Keogh. You could lose your arm."

"Never worry, Hunter. I'll still be around when you get out on the streets. Me and you got an appointment down the road. We'll see which side's stronger, *my* father or *yours*."

He never showed up in the jail again while I was there. I would hear patrolmen discussing him from time to time. On at least one occasion he called the dispatcher and told her he was on the ridge where he lived, waiting for an officer to kill. Nothing ever came of it, however. From time to time he would be sent off for a psychiatric evaluation.

It was pointless, though. Keogh learned early on of Tennessee's *Catch-22* laws. You cannot commit a person to a psychiatric hospital unless two doctors agree that the person is a threat to himself or to others. A judge must then sign the order. Keogh would simply deny all violent thoughts and walk out. In Tennessee, it is acceptable to believe you are a teapot as long as you are not a dangerous teapot.

I had been a patrolman for about six months the first

77

time I encountered Mike Keogh on the street. A complainant called the dispatcher and said that a white male was shooting a hunting bow in his front yard. She was afraid one of her dogs would be accidentally injured.

My heart was thumping as I drove up the small mountain. I knew where Keogh lived. I had made a point of finding out. Sure enough, he was standing in his front yard putting arrows into a target when I arrived. He had a unique target. It was from the police series of good guy/ bad guy targets. He was shooting at a police officer in full uniform. As I got out of the car, Keogh sunk a shaft into the target's left eye. He then put a second arrow dead center in the chest. I wondered if my body armor would stop an arrow. I was sure he could get off at least one, even if I was pumping him full of .38 hollow points.

"Hello, Officer Hunter. Pleasant evening, isn't it?"

"So far, it is." I flinched inwardly as he put another arrow to the string and buried it in the forehead of the target. My hand slowly dropped and unsnapped my holster. His eyes were burning into my hand as he turned.

"Don't worry. Now isn't the time, Officer Hunter."

"What if I decide that now *is* the time?" I was suddenly angry. "You have a lethal weapon in your hand. I can't think of a person in the world who wouldn't be happy to see me empty my weapon into you!"

"That won't happen," he said smiling, "because you're too *good*. That's why your side will lose in the end. It would be the smart thing, but it wouldn't be the *right* thing. When you worry about right and wrong, you put yourself at the disadvantage."

"Your neighbors think you're endangering them with that bow. I agree. Put it away and do it now. *Don't* reach for another arrow!"

"Oh, I won't. That might tip the scales," he said. "You just might do what you've really wanted to do since the day you met me—at the hospital."

I left shaken. I had no idea that he remembered our first brief encounter. Keogh put away the weapon and went inside, but the complainant found her dogs dead the next morning, their throats cut. The woman had learned her lesson, though. She did not complain. I got my information from an informant who first extracted an oath of secrecy that I would not tell Keogh how I came to know.

I felt shaken and out of control at the thoughts that had gone through my mind when I was talking to Keogh. Looking up an older and more experienced officer, I told him the story.

"It crossed my mind to kill him right there," I said. "It's frightening to think I don't have any more control than that."

"Sure it is, but you *didn't* shoot him. The difference between you and Keogh is principle. He apparently understands it very well. He's running a psychological bluff on you."

"It's frightening to think there's a guy out there who can take you apart with his hands."

"Come on, Hunter. You don't take people down with brute strength. You've fought guys as strong as Keogh. You took them with superior training. You've let this man grow into something he isn't. Unless, of course, you really do believe he's the Devil, or some dragon out of hell."

"No, of course not, but it *scares* me."

"Well, then welcome to the human race. He scared you, but you went after him anyway. We're *all* scared, Hunter," the older officer said.

"I guess you're right."

I did not think about Keogh again for two years, at least not when I was awake. He would sometimes slip into my nightmares. . . .

It was around 11:00 P.M. when the dispatcher sent me to a Clinton Highway nightspot on a disturbance call. I rolled in, backed up by another unit. The bouncer, an ex-outlaw biker, was standing at the door. At 220 pounds he had little trouble keeping order. He was clearly frightened that night.

"What's the problem, Bobby?"

"Got two guys in here. They won't let the dancer come off the stage, and they won't let my other customers leave. It's the two guys wearing sports coats."

The two sat quietly at a table. They were neatly dressed. Most Clinton Highway denizens are in work clothes. They were a little bigger than average, but they did not appear too menacing to me.

"They don't look like much to me, Bobby. You can't handle white-collar drunks?" I asked good-naturedly.

"Hunter, that guy in the plaid jacket almost made me piss in my pants when I looked him in the eyes. I don't know who or what he is, but he ain't *right*."

The other officer and I approached the table, watching the two closely. The one in the plaid coat had his back to me. "We need to see the two of you outside," I told them.

They complied quietly, and when they stood it was obvious that both were very drunk. The other officer took the one in the plaid sports jacket. I did not get a look at his face.

"What's the charge?" My prisoner asked as I was patting him down.

"Public drunkenness," I replied, taking his wallet out and flipping it open. "Keogh is an unusual name. You know Mike Keogh?"

"My brother," he replied. "That's him your friend's shakin' down."

Glancing out of the corner of my eye, I saw him. He had lost forty pounds and was cleanshaven. Panic hit me as I realized that I had walked up on him without realizing it.

"No need to call for help," Mike Keogh said. "If I was gonna fight, it would have been over by now. I scared the piss out of that bouncer, though." He laughed. It was an ugly laugh.

"Haven't seen you in a while, Mike," I said, sitting down to book him at the jail.

"I been up in Virginia at a private clinic," he said. "They've been trying to remove my delusions. We know they're not delusions, though. Don't we, Hunter?"

"I'm not in the mood, Keogh. Enough is enough. You're never going to be helped until you admit you need help." I went on with my paperwork.

"Pretend if you want," he said smiling, "but I know. I've been saving you for years. You're the only one who really knows me. You got the spiritual gift."

"I've got good cop instincts. Nothing more, nothing less."

"Have it your way, but when the time comes, it'll be *glorious*."

About a year later another patrolman stopped me. "Did you hear about Mike Keogh?"

"No, what happened?" My heart began to thump.

"He got drunk and hit a tree this morning. He was killed instantly. I don't know about you, but I'll breathe a little easier when I run that beat from now on."

My dragon was dead, killed in a mundane traffic accident. I *did* breathe easier. Sometimes, though, waking up from a nightmare, I think of him. Rationally, I know that he was a sick and deluded man who touched the superstitious child within me. Down on a gut level, though, I know what he was. He was evil incarnate. There are others like him out there, waiting.

13

A Child by the Side
of the Road

"**B**aker 10, I-75 at Emory Road. Check a child by the side of the road. The child will be with an adult male who appears to be 10-58."

"Well, it's started," I told Ron Aaron, the reserve who was riding with me. "The first drunk of the shift."

In a few minutes we rolled up to the intersection. There beside the road a tall, lanky individual was stretched out, an empty quart beer bottle beside him. Behind the man, huddled against the evening chill, was a small blond child of perhaps five, watching over him as if standing guard. He surveyed us as we approached with startling blue eyes that seemed to have the wisdom of the ages in them.

"Hello, little man," I said. "How are you tonight?"

"I'm fine, but my daddy got a little tired. He's takin' a nap. When he wakes up, we'll be goin' on to Florida." His voice had the lilt of the hills in it, but West Virginia, not Tennessee, I guessed.

"Looks like your daddy's not feeling well," I said. "This officer is going to take you to that little market over there and buy you a hot dog and soda while I check on your daddy."

"No thanks," he spoke like a miniature adult. "I'm not hungry. I'll just wait here until my daddy rests up."

"Go with the officer," I said gently, but firmly.

Reluctantly, he got up and followed the reserve officer. I knew Aaron would take him to the back of the store where he could not see what was happening. I checked the man's breathing and color. Everything appeared normal, except for the overpowering odor of alcohol coming from his breath. He was dog drunk.

"Get up." I nudged him with my toe.

"Wha . . . whatta *you* want," he said, sitting up.

"Stand up, you're under arrest for public drunkenness." I wondered how long it would take him to miss the child.

"I ain't drunk. Go away and leave me alone." He started to lie down, but I reached and picked him up by his collar. Of course, he swung at me. He was a true mountain man in that respect. Whirling him around, I brought his arm up behind him and pinned him to a telephone pole.

"Mister, I'm already upset with you. Don't swing at me again!"

"I ain't done nothin'." He whined. "Me and my boy. . . . Where's my boy?"

"I wondered when you'd remember you're supposed to be a grown man looking out for a little child," I snapped. "We've got him in custody. You won't be in a position to endanger him for awhile."

Two cruisers pulled up behind me. The captain took one look at my face and told the other officer to take custody. A good supervisor knows when one of his officers has reached a crisis point.

"Write the warrant," the captain said. "Upchurch will transport."

"All right, but pull over to the other side of the lot. I don't want the little boy to see his daddy in the cruiser."

Inside I found Aaron and the little boy sitting at a table. An untouched hot dog sat in front of the child, though he was sipping the drink.

"Aren't you hungry?" I asked.

"Where's my daddy?"

"He isn't feeling well. We're going to have some people look at him. I'm going to take you to a place where there are a lot of children to play with, until someone can come and pick you up."

"You're gonna put him in jail, ain't cha?"

"For a while," I said, swallowing a lump in my throat. "What's your name?"

"Robert Crawford, from West V'ginia."

"How old are you, Robert?" I asked.

"I'm five. My daddy'll be all right in a little while. He's not a bad man."

"I know that, Robert, but the road's a dangerous place at night. Your daddy's in no condition to take care of you. I can't leave you on the road. Bring your hot dog and soda. We're going for a ride."

We drove south on I-75, the pale light of the dashboard reflecting on Robert's face. He had not shed a tear. Suddenly I was struck by his uncanny resemblance to my son Paris, sleeping safely in his bed a few miles from where I had found Robert. I thought of Paris, alone by the side of the road, standing watch.

"Do you watch television, Robert?" I asked.

He nodded affirmatively.

"Do you watch 'He-man?' I have a son your age, and he watches 'He-man.'"

Once more he nodded affirmatively but did not speak.

"Do you have any 'He-man' toys, Robert?"

"No, but Momma says I might get some for Christmas."

I looked at the ragged and dirty clothes. Christmas, I was certain, would be a lean affair at Robert's house.

At the shelter I signed the paper, stating that Robert was in protective custody. In Tennessee a social worker can only take custody of a child for twenty-four hours, a police officer for forty-eight hours. During that time a juvenile court judge must act.

"Robert, I'll be back in the morning. These are nice people here. They'll take good care of you."

"Take good care of my daddy," the child said. I did not answer. I could not.

I did not go to bed after work the next morning. Two hours after my shift ended, I was at the Department of Human Services. The worker took notes, giving me puzzled glances. Police officers do not personally involve themselves in such cases.

"What will happen now?" I asked.

"We'll contact his family and try to get a responsible person to come and pick him up," she said.

"*Responsible person*," I growled. "You mean like the people who let a drunk hitchhike down the interstate with a five-year-old? Come on, you can do better than that. You'd do better than that for a pup!"

"Officer, I appreciate your concern, but I think you need some rest. You know as well as I do that the law is the law. We *both* abide by it."

"I'm sorry I snapped at you. I didn't realize I was so upset."

"Go home and get some sleep. We'll call you for the hearing."

A few minutes later I was at K-Mart, standing in the checkout lane with new clothes and a 'He-man' figurine. I bought clothes to fit my son, and they were exactly the right size.

At the door of the shelter, the woman looked at my uniform and let me in. I removed the figurine and handed her the clothes. Robert came quietly into the room and stood there. I picked him up on my lap and unwrapped the toy. He looked it over dutifully and thanked me.

"Robert, we're working things out for you. I want you to enjoy yourself and not worry. Your family will be after you in a little while."

"Will you see my daddy?" he asked.

"Yes, I'm going to court with him this afternoon."

"Tell him I love him," he said like a little man.

"I'll do that, Robert," I said, choking back the tears that were forming around the rims of my eyes. No child so young should be so old.

At the jail I interviewed Robert's father. His attitude was surly, even sober. "If you'd left us alone, me and the boy'd be in Florida by now."

"You'd be in Florida, or your son would be in the hands of a child molester," I almost shouted. "I didn't come to argue with you. I want some information so I can care for your son!"

"I'll take care of my own son. They can't hold me but a few hours for bein' drunk."

"Wrong," I told him. "We're going to court in a little while, and I'm going to explain the circumstances to a judge. If I can help it, you'll never abuse that child again."

The man glared at my back—still unrepentant—as I left. That afternoon he was sentenced to fifteen days for public drunkenness. I left the courtroom and went to see a lawyer who was also a close friend. He sat quietly, tapping the desk with his pencil as I laid out the case.

"What exactly do you want?" He asked when I had stopped talking.

"I want you to draw up some kind of temporary order granting me custody until we can get this into the courts."

"We both know that's absurd. Go home and go to bed. You're on the verge of collapse right now. The courts will give that child back to his mother. It's as simple as that."

"No! I've got some powerful friends in this county. I'll pull some strings. I'm not going to let anyone endanger that child again."

He sat staring at me. He knew how I felt about "powerful friends" and "political influence." Ashamed of my outburst, I shrugged and looked out the window.

"Look, Hunter, you're emotionally involved. Don't feel like the Lone Ranger. It happens to all of us. Go home and get some sleep."

By the time I contacted the Department of Human Services and found out that Robert's mother was on her way and that the hearing would take place at 8:00 A.M., it was too late to go to bed. I had been up for thirty-six hours. Somehow I made it through the shift, rehearsing in my mind an impassioned plea to the judge to allow Robert to stay here.

There was no doubt in my mind, though, what the judge would do the next morning. He was bound by laws, as I was bound by laws. Every good cop—even in his blackest rage—knows that the difference between him and the slime is obedience to the law. Still, I was prepared to go down fighting because I have never understood any other way.

The next morning—after two days without sleep—I was sworn in at juvenile court. The Assistant District Attorney elicited the bare essentials of the story from me, as a good prosecutor always does. In the back of the room Robert's mother sobbed. She was a plain woman of perhaps forty, with straight black hair and no makeup. I took her for a member of one of the Holiness sects that abound in the Appalachians.

Robert's father was brought in wearing the orange jumpsuit of the Knox County jail. He replied sulkily to the judge's questions but denied nothing. It was still his position that everything would have worked out well if I had not interfered while he was resting by the road.

"Does anyone have any further statements or comments?" the judge asked.

"I do, Your Honor."

"Proceed, Officer."

"Your Honor, this child was placed in extreme danger, both by an irresponsible father and by a mother who obviously cannot influence the situation. It is obvious that Robert's father shows no remorse, sees nothing wrong with what he did. I believe the child will be in danger if returned to his family. I ask that the State of Tennessee take custody of Robert Crawford for his own protection. There are people—and I am one of them—who will gladly assume the responsibility of seeing that this child is cared for properly. Thank you."

I sat down, drained. The look of sympathy on the judge's face told me that it had been a hopeless plea. I had tried, though. I could hear Robert's mother sobbing even louder in the background.

"Thank you, Officer," the judge said. "I agree that the child was placed in extreme jeopardy. However, when a child can be returned to his family, it is best to do so.

"I am, however, remanding Robert Crawford to the care and custody of the West Virginia Department of Human Services. He will remain at home, but under the supervision of a case worker. At no time will Robert's father be allowed to leave the house with the child." He turned to the man.

"As for you, Sir, rest assured that had you come before my court, instead of General Sessions, you would stay in jail longer than fifteen days. You have committed a heinous act. Do you have anything to say on your behalf?"

The man shook his head, looking down at the table. A moment later he was escorted away by a court officer. He did not look at his wife during the entire hearing.

"Your Honor, may I have permission to visit Robert and tell him that his mother will be picking him up?"

"You may do so. Also, the court takes note of a job well done on your part, Officer Hunter."

On the way out, Robert's mother and a man who appeared to be a clergyman tried to speak to me. I pushed past them, not trusting myself to be civil.

A half hour later I had Robert on my lap. He was wearing his new clothes and had the toy under his arm. "Your mother will be picking you up in a little while, Robert. You're going home. There's something I want you to always remember, though, wherever you go. When you need help, go to a policeman. We are your friends, not your enemy."

"What about my daddy?" he asked.

"He's fine, Robert. He'll be coming along behind you in a few days."

"My daddy's not a bad man. He justs drinks too much sometimes," the blond child with the startling blue eyes said.

"I know, Robert." My eyes were stinging, and I knew I was losing my grip. "I'm leaving now. I want you to have a good life, Robert."

"Bye." He put his arms around my neck and kissed me on the cheek. "I know you had to put my daddy in jail. I'm not mad at ya'."

Outside, I leaned into the steering wheel, composing myself. Police officers do not like to weep in public. It is bad for the image. At home I dropped gratefully into bed and slept for twelve hours.

The next Christmas I took Robert's address off his father's arrest report and mailed a package of "He-man" toys. It was something I could not even bring myself to discuss with my wife at the time. The wound was too fresh, too deep.

I included no return address, no note. Robert would know where the package had come from. Even if his father drank up everything else that year, Robert still got something for Christmas.

14

Bein' Whipped Is Better Than Nothin' at All

He was nineteen the first time I saw him. Tall, gangly, stringy blond hair, and drunk out of his mind. He had come home drunk and was breaking up the furniture. As the cruiser pulled up, he looked out the front door of the trailer, jumped off the porch, and tried to run away at a drunken stagger. Sprinting across the yard, I caught him by the collar. As he tried to turn and swing at me, I spun around and put an elbow in his gut.

By the time help arrived, I had him cuffed, but he had not calmed down. He cursed, kicked, and screamed. As we stuffed him in the cruiser, he kicked me in the chest. He seemed to be having a marvelous time.

It was my last shift as a reserve officer, a Friday night. The following Monday I went to work full-time as a jailer, as do all Knox County officers. Over the next two years I became well acquainted with Tim Hodge. You could expect him at least once a month, and it was always the same. He would come in battered and bruised from having tried to punch it out with cops, who generally take it seriously when you try to hurt them.

He always left, however, with no hard feelings and never complained. Your typical barroom brawler has a grudge against the world. He hates everyone, most especially the officers who interfere with his "right" to behave as he pleases. He will generally file complaints of brutality or whatever else. Tim never did this.

After two years as a jailer, I hit the streets of north Knox County as a patrol officer. Tim lived in a small trailer park on Clinton Highway. I had put him in jail—kicking and fighting—several times when I finally caught on. Despite his ferocious manner, he had never actually hurt anyone. No matter how clumsy you are, if you are serious about mayhem, eventually you will hurt someone.

It was a Friday when the call came in. He was sitting on the front steps of the trailer. As soon as I pulled up, he rose and staggered toward me. "I guess you've come for some action," he said. "You'd better call for help."

"Naw, I haven't come for action and I don't need any help. I'm not going to put you in jail."

"Yes, by God! You'll put me in jail, or I'll whip your stinkin' ass." He stood glaring at me.

"No, you won't do that. You don't *want* to do that."

He came at me running. I spun him around and caught him in a bear hug, pinning his arms. He struggled for a few moments, then went limp. He began to sob as I pulled him over and sat him on the porch.

"As soon as you calm down, you can go inside and hit the rack," I told him.

"I can't," he sobbed. "I'm broke, and she threw me out again."

"I'm sure your mother will let you in when you calm down."

"She's not my real mother. My real mother left me when I was four. The welfare people paid Thelma to raise me. The payments stopped when I turned eighteen. Now she puts me out when I don't pay her."

"Is that why you go to jail so often, to have a place to sleep?"

"No, I can sleep outside in the summer. I go to jail because it's the only time anybody ever notices that I'm alive. Bein' whipped is better than nothin' at all, Mister Hunter."

I turned away from his tear-stained face, momentarily. You cannot look upon such truth and pain, any more than you can look directly at the sun. Most of us mask our loneliness, our fears. Tim Hodge hit me in the face with his that night.

"Go get in my car, Tim."

He complied, still sobbing. I drove him to a motel on my beat and called in a favor from the night clerk. The next afternoon I returned to pick him up. He was shaky, but sober. In front of a restaurant I stopped and handed him ten dollars. He stared at it, then at me.

"What's this for?"

"You're going to buy me a hamburger. If I pay for it, word will get out that I'm going soft. You'll pay me next Friday when you get your first check."

"I don't have a job," he said.

"Yes, you do, and it's a lousy job. You'll be cleaning up cars, sweeping, and anything else you're told to do. You'll stay sober because if you don't, I'll kick your young ass up around your shoulders. I told this guy you're dependable, and you're going to *be* dependable. Understand?"

"Yes, *Sir!*" he said with a crooked smile.

Clinton Highway was quieter the next few months. The car dealer was pleased with Tim's work and sold him a car on credit. I took him for a driving test, and he was mobile for the first time in his life, able to escape the confines of his narrow world.

He called me one afternoon and asked me to meet him at the restaurant where I had bought him the meal. I was treated to the best the place had to offer. As we were finishing up, he sprang a surprise on me.

"That job you got me, Mister Hunter. . . ."

"Yeah?"

"I'm going to give it up," he said, lowering his eyes.

"Why?"

"Because I got a better job," he laughed. "Fooled you, didn't I! You thought I was fallin' off the wagon. You ain't mad, are ya? I know you got it for me."

"Tim, I couldn't be more pleased. The time comes when

a man has to fly on his own. If you need help, yell. Otherwise, you are now your own man."

Months later he approached me at my usual breakfast spot. He had a thin, washed-out blonde in tow and acted the way a child does when he has accomplished something important.

"Mister Hunter, I want you to meet Candy. I'm gonna marry her."

"Hello, Candy," I said. "It's nice to meet you."

I bought breakfast for them and tried not to stare at Candy's arms. The needle tracks, raw and red, were visible every time her sleeve slid back past the elbows. After they left, I called Records. That afternoon I went out to where Tim was working.

"Something wrong, Mister Hunter?" I had long before told him to call me by my first name, but he stubbornly refused to do it. He was sweating from the backbreaking labor he did, unloading produce trucks.

"Yes, and I don't know how to say it, Tim."

"Is it about Candy?"

"Yes, it is."

"I figured you'd check her out. I know she used to be a whore, and I don't mind, Mister Hunter. I love her."

"I don't care about her sex life," I snapped. "She's a junkie, Tim. A junkie only loves the needle."

"I can help her, Mister Hunter. Nobody's past savin'. *You* told me that. Look at me. Look what you done for me." Tears welled in his eyes. "I never had nobody of my own before."

"All right, Tim. A man has to make his own decisions. I want you to remember something, though. If this doesn't work out, it's no reflection on you. Don't throw away everything you've done for yourself."

It was three months later when I walked into the jail one evening and found Tim sitting on the bench. He was drunk and badly battered. He dropped his eyes as I approached. I bit back an angry thought.

"Come back here in the hall, Tim."

"Her ex-husband showed up last night," Tim began to

sob. "He brought some dope in and told her she could have it if she'd throw me out. It was like I was a dog or somethin'. All she could see was the dope. He beat me up and she . . . she told me not to come back." He wept uncontrollably.

The roller coaster ride had started. When her ex-husband was gone, Tim would be allowed to return. When the man showed up with narcotics, Tim was out again. It was only a matter of time before Tim's arrests for drunken driving began. He was caught twice in one month. The second time he was given forty-five days.

While he was in jail, I talked to some friends and got him into an alcohol rehabilitation program. A month later he was clean again, working at his old job. Shortly afterward, Candy called him. She was about to lose her apartment. Tim went back, caught up the rent, and was doing well when her ex-husband returned. The scene was repeated over and over again.

He was on the final spiral down when I saw him the last time, standing in front of a Clinton Highway bar, tossing a red poker chip from Alcoholics Anonymous. He dropped his eyes as I pulled up.

"I'm not drinking, Mister Hunter. I'm working here. They pay me to watch the lot, make sure nobody bothers the cars."

"This isn't a good place for you, Tim. You know that."

"Work's hard to find," he said with a shrug. "I'm goin' to A.A. twice a day now. I'll be all right. Don't you worry."

It was the last time I saw him alive.

"Mike wanted me to call and tell you that Tim Hodge was just killed on Clinton Highway," Brenda Upchurch said. "He was run over by a car."

Later in the evening I talked to the state trooper who had worked the accident. "It was kosher," he said. "Hodge ran right out in front of the car. Was he one of your snitches?"

"Yeah, you might say that," I told him.

"He had this in his pocket," the trooper said. "Does it

mean anything?" He was holding a red poker chip.

"Not now," I told him.

The next day I signed the book at the funeral home. The coffin stood at the back of the chapel. There was a single flower arrangement. I had sent it. The coffin, of course, could not be opened. All the king's men could not put Tim Hodge back the way he was.

"You're the only one who showed up today," a funeral home employee told me. "This guy must not have had too many friends."

"No, the only time he ever got any attention was when he was drunk," I said, walking back to the car.

A few days later I heard some officers joking about Tim's death and that the world would be a better place without him. I felt a flare of anger, then subdued it. I had made similar comments.

Eventually I pieced together Tim's last evening. As he stood watching the cars, his wife pulled in with her ex-husband. Taunting words were hurled at Tim. He went inside and tossed down several drinks as fast as he could. Moments later he ran in front of a car.

He said it pretty well. "Bein' whipped is better than nothin' at all."

15

As Long as His Death Had Meaning

I t was one of those muggy southern nights that make a mockery of modern technology. The air was so humid it was almost a mist, and the plastic-covered Kevlar body armor I was wearing held the sweat against my skin until it puddled and ran down my body. When my misery became unbearable, I would turn on the air conditioning, which would immediately chill me until I turned it off and started the cycle again.

It was the kind of long, hot night for which the South is known, the kind of night when tempers flare and poor people in tinbox trailers open all the windows seeking relief, then call the cops because their neighbors are playing music too loudly for them to hear their own.

Despite the heat and flaring tempers, the night seemed to drag on and on. Most—but not all—were too lethargic to cause any real problems. Aside from "loud music" calls, the only thing of note that night had been a petty larceny at an all-night market.

"He walked right in, bold as could be, without sayin' a word. He picked up a case of Miller's and walked out the door like I wasn't even here," the frustrated assistant manager told me. Even when there are only two employees in these little markets, one will be the manager,

97

the other the assistant manager.

"They should drop an atom bomb on that trailer park," he said.

"This store would be at ground zero. The blast would get you too," I reminded him with heavy irony. It was lost in his indignation. A skinny man with old, black plastic-framed glasses, he would not be deflected from his rage. I waited while he vented his frustration.

"You got any idea how much money I lose from theft? They're all a bunch of thieves, and they're raisin' another generation of thieves. They come in and one gets my attention while the rest gulp down drinks. They smoke dope in my bathroom and tear up the fixtures. I'm tellin' you, they should bomb that trailer park right out of existence!"

I did not bother to correct him. It was not *a* trailer park, but *several* trailer parks. They had grown, sprawling out over a small valley just off Highway 33, until they *looked* like one large trailer park.

In the early seventies a nearby mobile home manufacturer had an idea. How about a small, controlled trailer park with "quality" trailers and people, a family place? Taking advantage of a lack of zoning regulations in the county, he started a small community. Right next to him, another park opened. Later businessmen were not as concerned with "quality." They dug a lot of septic tanks and put up power poles.

People looking for permanence generally do not linger too long in mobile home parks. As the early residents moved on to their own lots or to permanent housing, a new breed moved in. Soon there were rattletrap cars parked everywhere, yapping dogs, and a thriving narcotics business. The owners soon found, like slumlords everywhere, that it is cheaper to rent to people who seldom complain. Transients and those who have never known better will accept things that others will not tolerate.

By the mid-'80s the children of earlier residents were renting space, unaware that any other type of lifestyle existed. The parks continued to grow, eventually collapsing inward until there appeared to be only one giant park consisting of hundreds of trailers.

In 1983 another ingredient was added. Having filled up all its projects, the government began to search for new housing. The trailer park owners offered a solution. Now, in addition to the regular residents, who for the most part worked for a living, were added the hard-core unemployables.

The situation deteriorated. The welfare recipients—some third generation—were used to a city environment. "Country living" bored them. They began to acquire old cars, adding to the already cluttered streets. It became a slum in miniature.

This was part of my beat when I went on patrol in 1983. A sprawling community, for the most part it consisted of rusty, run-down, substandard trailers. Hard-core unemployables were lumped in like sardines, along with the resentful working class people who had preceded them.

"When is the Sheriff's Department gonna do something? That's what I wanna know." the assistant manager asked.

"What do you suggest?" I had listened about as long as I was inclined to listen.

"Well, you could put more men out here, for one thing," he said lamely.

"Call your county commissioner and tell him that," I said pleasantly. "He'll listen to you. Unfortunately you taxpayers have been telling the commission that you don't want to spend money on law enforcement. We could use twice the officers we have now."

"I know, I know," he said, raising his hands, "you do the best you can. I wasn't tryin' to get personal."

"I know. Give me a description, and I'll see if I can locate the thief." We both knew what my chances were.

"He was young—nineteen or so—dark brown hair and eyes. He was about six feet, and lanky. He was wearing a yellow T-shirt and a red ballcap."

"I ought to notice those colors," I told the clerk.

Finishing my report, I cruised through the mobile home parks. There was no chance that my thief would be out,

99

but the assistant manager would be watching. If I did not make a token search, he would complain about me. I was greeted with hostile glances and comments, even from the small children. The park is a place where kids do not make heroes of cops.

A little later I cruised through the big shopping center at Halls, running out the teenagers congregating on the lot. It was apparently too hot, even for the usual defiant high school students. They moved along without comment. I was about to head out for the back roads when the dispatcher sent me back to the park I had just left. "Baker 10, 10-59 in progress. Possible 10-81."

I hit the blue lights and sirens, heading back. The dispatcher had said "fight in progress and possible cutting scrape." There probably would not be anything to it. Still, you never know. My adrenalin was pumping as I pulled in to the cul-de-sac where the trailer was located. The crowd had a bad look to it. Neanderthals probably formed the same type of crowds when there was trouble in the caves.

I approached the aging trailer with rust stains running down the sides. There was obviously no fight in progress. The participants probably had heard me coming and fled. Then I saw the feet lying on the floor just inside the open trailer door. Drawing my weapon, I stepped through the door, covering the trailer inside. A pretty blonde girl with remarkably blue eyes was staring calmly at me.

"Tommy cut my husband," she said, matter-of-factly. "They went outside to fight. Then Jerry stumbled back in and said that Tommy had cut him."

Her husband lay sprawled on the floor, arms and legs awry, eyes opened and glassed over, staring into eternity. The crimson stain on his yellow T-shirt was already turning brown as the blood dried. There was a small puddle on the linoleum, but he had not lived long enough to bleed very much. I lifted his shirt and saw a small triangular stab wound, just under his left nipple. The wound had probably been made with a pocket knife, rather than a dagger.

"Baker 10, I need an ambulance, a homicide officer, and at least one other patrol unit to help me secure the scene. I have a homicide here."

I went to the door and told the crowd to stay put until someone could question them. There was no need for the instructions, though. This was definitely better than television. I took an initial report from the wife to help out the homicide officer.

"My husband came in with a case of beer earlier," she said calmly. "Him and Tommy started drinkin' and listenin' to some old records we bought at a flea market. You know, old fashioned stuff, like the Beatles. . . ."

I was momentarily stung. To hear the Beatles called "old-fashioned" was very painful. "Is that your husband's ball cap on the table?"

"Yeah, he was wearin' it when he come home with the beer."

The mystery of the beer thief was solved. A yellow T-shirt and a red ballcap. Miller cans were scattered all over the trailer.

"Go on," I said.

"They was listenin' to these old records. There was one Tommy wanted to hear, a Marty Robbins album, but Jerry wouldn't put it on. They got to arguin'. Jerry said it was his home, and if Tommy didn't like it, he could get out.

"Tommy said somethin' back—I couldn't hear what it was—and Jerry smacked him in the face. Tommy run out the door with Jerry beatin' on the back of his head. I couldn't see what was happenin', not until Jerry stumbled in."

"Anyone else here when it happened?"

She named two people. I went out, and they verified her story. Tommy was trying to get away, but Jerry kept pounding him. Jerry was bad about that, they said. A real animal when he was drinking.

Another patrolman arrived, followed by the homicide officer and the girl's family. I had the patrolman herd all the family members to a back room. When the dead man's family arrived, I sent them to the back also in order to preserve the scene while the homicide officer was collecting his evidence. The trailer was filled with the eerie glow of the camera's strobe light, freezing the scene in time.

101

A commotion broke out in the rear of the trailer. I found the girl's father and father-in-law shoving each other, red-faced and angry.

"Don't you ever say nothin' like that about my daughter again!"

"It's the truth, ain't it? She kept that other boy sniffin' around her like a dog in heat. She couldn't make up her mind what she wanted. Now my boy is dead!"

"Let me tell *both* of you something," I said, stepping into the room. "If I hear any more of this nonsense, I'll start loading my cruiser. Understand?"

They nodded sullenly. A few minutes later I saw them swapping a half pint of whiskey back and forth, their differences apparently forgotten. They had both lived in the trailer park a long time and would go on being neighbors when this was over.

"Well, I'm finished," the homicide investigator told the waiting ambulance crew. "You can take him on."

"Take him to the nearest hospital," his wife said.

"Sorry," I replied. "He has to be taken to University."

"Why?" she asked.

"Because all violent deaths have to be checked by the coroner."

"You mean he's *dead?*" she asked, as if a man who had lain in the same position unmoving for an hour could have been otherwise.

She began to scream a high piercing scream, but it did not last long. In a few minutes her mother had calmed her.

"Did the investigator tell you what they were fighting about?" the patrolman asked as the ambulance pulled away.

"The wife told me," I replied.

"Can you believe it?" the young patrolman asked. "He died over a record."

"Well, as long as his death had meaning," I said tiredly, "as long as it wasn't a trivial thing."

The girl and her mother were discussing practical matters as I left. They were debating whether or not she would be able to keep the trailer, or if she would have to find a cheaper place. I wondered where they would find a cheaper place than the trailer court.

As I was getting into the cruiser, I remembered the blood on the floor. I wondered who would clean it up. Would the girl do it? Would she make a single swipe of the mop and obliterate the last traces of her husband? Would the girl's mother-in-law do it as a final gesture of good will?

I wondered about that for a long time. I decided to ask the girl the next time I was at her trailer. There would be other calls there. Of that I was certain.

16

Some Say Love Is Like a Razor

The evening started out quietly, as do most interesting days. As beverage control officer for the Knox County Sheriff's Department, I was working the 3:00 P.M. to 11:00 P.M. shift. A couple of small grocery stores had become a little too liberal with their beer sales to young people, and I intended to stop long enough to read them the riot act. Then I'd spend the rest of the evening catching up on the seemingly endless mounds of paperwork piled on my desk.

At the time I was still relatively new to working in plainclothes as an investigator. Patrol officers say that most investigators will drive through a gun battle in progress, rather than get involved with something that will require a court day or working past shift change. I suppose I will always be a patrolman at heart.

"Baker 19," the dispatcher said, "and any unit that can assist, 10-83, 10-85, in progress." The codes meant "domestic problem" and "disturbance." The location was a remote area, so I told the dispatcher I would back up the unit that was en route. Most such problems come to nothing, but a domestic dispute is potentially one of the deadliest calls an officer can handle. I did not want the officer, a former shiftmate and personal friend, out there alone.

The majority of domestic disputes occur at home, of course. Such a call requires that an officer trample the sacred ground of someone's castle, that the residing monarch be challenged on his home ground. If the parties are drunk or drugged enough, they will sometimes resist. This is why a domestic call is so dangerous, particularly for a lone officer.

There are no winners in most domestic disputes. When tempers cool, the officer who arrested the husband or wife becomes the villain and complaints are filed, often by the complaining party, against the officer. Even when someone is convicted of domestic violence, judges are prone to leniency because jail time means an individual cannot support the family he has been abusing.

Cops hate domestic disputes.

I arrived in the general vicinity, deciding to wait for Joey Cook to arrive. When the dispatcher advised us that the situation was deteriorating, I moved on in. Stopping at the bottom of the driveway, I spoke to the complainant. She said her sister was being physically abused in a nearby garage apartment. As we talked, a bloodcurdling scream came from the apartment.

One thing an officer quickly learns is to distinguish between cries of frustration or rage and cries of pain and fear. "Unit 10, I'm going in." I ran toward the apartment, fully expecting to find a dead woman.

Drawing my weapon, I approached the door. The garage was built into the side of a hill, putting me nearly level with the door. There was no light burning inside, but I could see a large man bending over a bed. The woman on the bed was whimpering like an injured pup.

"You, inside, get your hands up where I can see them. Do it now!" My weapon was aimed at his chest.

As the man raised up, I could see the terror-stricken woman. Her face was tear-stained and her throat was bleeding, though it did not appear to be an arterial wound. Her eyes were affixed to his hand, and for the first time I saw the knife.

"Drop the weapon! Walk toward me with your hands out to your side. Do it now!"

His weapon hand dropped to his side, where he fumbled with something at his belt. I nearly shot him. You never get used to confronting armed assailants, no matter how often it happens.

"Damn it, I said keep your hands where I can see them!"

He paused, glaring, and walked toward the door. The knife was no longer visible. He had dropped it, or had stashed it somewhere on his person.

"Face down, spread-eagle on the ground. Do it now! Get your arms and legs spread out." In the light I saw that he was young, bearded, about six foot five inches and 230 pounds. I took the time to glance briefly at the woman's wound, while covering the suspect. She was cut just under her ear, but there was no arterial bleeding.

Never in my life have I ever seen such horror written on a human face. She dashed out of the room and ran down the hill sobbing as Joey Cook pulled into the driveway.

"Now," I said, positioning myself to search the man, "I'm going to search you. If you twitch while I'm doing it, I'll blow your brains out. Understand?"

"I understand," he mumbled.

As Joey approached, I pitched not one, but two, large lock-bladed knives towards him. The blade of one was covered with blood. He had placed the knife he was using to torture the girl into a leather sheath at his side. The bloody knife blade was as sharp as a razor. He had been pulling it, she later told me, across her throat, accusing her of infidelity and telling her that she was about to die.

Cook arrested the man on a preliminary charge of domestic violence. I did a "first officer" report and told the woman to go the hospital, then meet a homicide officer at the City–County Building. I headed in to attack my mounds of paperwork. It was a routine call for a patrol officer, and I thought no more about it.

A couple of hours later, I dropped off my "first officer" report at the homicide office. "That was a good lick, Hunter," Dan Stewart said, handing me his report on the aggravated assault charge. "You probably saved that woman's life, as I noted in the report."

"I appreciate the plug, Dan, but Joey Cook would have done what I did. I just got there first."

"She might have been dead. That's what she told me, anyway," he said with a shrug.

I made copies for my file and went back to my office. I was involved with sorting arrest reports when the knock came on my office door. Opening the door, I recognized a reporter.

"Officer Hunter, can I get a statement from you on this assault you worked a while ago?"

"You need to talk to Dan Stewart," I said. "He's working the case."

"I've already talked to him. Both he and the victim say you saved that woman's life. I just need a couple of quotes."

"It was just a routine call. Patrol officers do that sort of thing every day. I don't understand what the big deal is."

"Just a couple of quotes," he said.

I answered his questions, then promptly forgot about it. In fact, it seemed so routine and inconsequential at the time I did not even mention it to my wife. The next morning, however, I passed another officer. He gave me the "thumbs up" and said, "Good write-up."

Puzzled, I went to the news rack in front of the City–County Building. On the front page of the *Journal* were headlines that read: "Beverage Investigator Saves Woman's Life." The article went on to say how I had "volunteered" to undertake a dangerous call. In seven years I had never received a front page write-up.

The story ran on most of the radio stations that day. Friends called to congratulate me. Nobody wanted to hear my disclaimers. I was elected "Officer of the Month," given the Kiwanis Club humanitarian award, and invited to speak on a radio talk show about domestic violence. Like the song says, "When you're hot, you're hot."

I was definitely beginning to enjoy the publicity and attention. I was a short step away from believing I had done something noteworthy. My wife pointed out that I was getting a swelled head. She also pointed out that I had never been overly impressed by awards, because I had always said that an officer's real reward is to have honorably discharged his duties. It is hard to listen to reason, though, when the sound of cheering is thundering in your ears.

The courtroom was crowded the day of the preliminary hearing. The courtroom is *always* crowded, but I was sure they were all there for *my* hearing. I had all but forgotten I was only a witness in the case.

The media was there, and I was going over what I intended to say. Just before court, however, Ted Burnett, the assistant attorney general, called Dan Stewart and me aside. "We're going to have to retire the warrant on this aggravated assault," he said.

"How can you even consider that," I growled. "He was *torturing* that woman, cutting her throat a little at a time with a razor-sharp knife."

"I know," Ted told us, "but he just married the victim. His lawyer has a marriage certificate."

"It doesn't matter," I said, grasping at straws. "It's a felony. We can still prosecute."

"Right," Burnett said, "and probably get him indicted on your testimony. Here's the bottom line, though. We'll never get a conviction. Even his lawyer doesn't like this. But we can't win, Hunter. It's as simple as that."

"I know," I said tiredly. "We won't need her testimony the next time. She'll be dead."

The case was called, and the man and his new bride came forward. She would not look me in the eye. Looking at her, I remembered the sheer terror on her face the day of the assault and wondered how she could risk such pain again. They left arm in arm.

A romantic, I suppose, would think of this incident as an example of true love overcoming pain. I saw it as the case of a born victim going to her fate. I was wrong, though. He left his new wife shortly afterward and I learned through street sources that he soon moved in with a new woman.

Some say love is like a razor, or at least a sharp knife.

17

Haunted Streets

Southern cops work haunted streets and are on intimate terms with the ghosts who inhabit them. This is something they do not warn you about at the academy. There is no course entitled "Ghosts and How to Deal With Them." Neither is it covered in the criminal codes.

In fact, no rookie ever learns about ghosts from his training officer. The subject is never discussed, but every southern cop learns about them and learns to cope in his own way. A big-city cop probably has his own ghosts, but he can ask for a transfer to another part of the city. It does not take long to fill up a rural beat, however.

I acquired my first ghost out on I-75, one morning around 1:00 A.M. I had stopped to assist a harried state trooper. The victim had been run over by a truck, her body smeared along the interstate for one hundred yards with no more dignity than the 'possums that litter the state's highways and byways.

"I've got measurements," the trooper said, "but I can't find any identification. Take a look—if you don't mind— before I let the ambulance crew in to clean up."

I have been asked by friends, "How do you deal with a dismembered body?"

A dismembered body is easier to cope with than a mutilated body because it has no evident connection to a living human being. A dismembered body is *abstracted*, disassociated from reality. It is harder for me to gut a rabbit or a deer than to view such a scene. A mutilated body is another story and has no place in this story.

Walking for fifty yards eastbound, I stepped over body parts—skull fragments here, an arm there, blood mixed with diesel fuel. Finally I found what I was looking for. At first it looked like a pink rag. Closer examination revealed a small clutch purse, apparently the woman's only valuables. Inside was a tube of lipstick—new and freshly used—a comb, a pair of cheap gold earrings, and a card showing that she had been released one day earlier from a mental institution in another city.

The purse held no money. It seemed likely that she had spent whatever she had for the lipstick. Her last concern was not food, but a splash of color to liven the world. I quickly blinked back tears before the approaching trooper could see me.

"Thanks," he said as I handed it to him and walked back to my cruiser. A human being should not die alone in the dark, especially a human being who has spent her last money, not on food, but on a small personal vanity. Such a *human* gesture.

There was no picture on the identification card and certainly not enough of the woman to form a mental image, but I knew what she looked like. And I knew she would be here when I passed again.

Those you have known can be put to rest. If you have talked with them, laughed with them, they do not linger. It is those who die alone in the dark who will not go away. The next time I went that way, she was there. A tired blonde woman in her middle thirties wearing a blue print dress. Her mouth was a splash of scarlet. She stood by the road, silent and accusing.

The ghosts can sometimes be shared, though not discussed.

One night I backed up another officer on a "shots fired"

112

call in a small community park. There was nothing to the call, so he broke out his thermos of Colombian coffee and we had a cup. He stood there, a man in his early thirties, hair streaked with white. It crossed my mind how quickly this job turns young cops into old ones.

"I found a body here one night," he said, lighting a cigarette. "A rape victim."

"Oh, yeah?" I lit up myself, remembering that I was supposed to stop smoking this week. I had promised my wife.

"She was under that shed over there, on the picnic table. Twenty years old. She was wearing nothing but a red sweater, lying on her back with her legs spread, just the way the rapist left her. I covered her with my coat. She was somebody's daughter."

A chill began to vibrate up my spine.

"The bad thing was," he threw down his cigarette and stepped on it, "the coroner said she died from exposure. If I had come through an hour earlier, she could have been saved. I had worked a wreck, though, early in the shift and was tied up."

"You had no way of knowing." By that time I was shaking visibly and hoping he would not notice.

"I know," he said, "but have you ever noticed how life and death seem to hang on things that we can't control?"

He got back into his cruiser, and I watched him drive away. There was no need to look behind me. I knew she was there, lying on her back, legs spread, eyes glassed over, staring into eternity.

How horrible to be violated and left on a picnic table for the world to see your shame, to scream for help and have no relief. I shuddered and got into my cruiser without looking back. I knew I would never drive through the park again without seeing her.

The joy of police work remains with a good cop forever, but it is never quite the same after the ghosts begin to turn up. Here an old woman was run over by a car as she went to the mailbox. There a child perished in a trailer fire. Down the road a wealthy farmer hanged himself from the rafters of his red and white barn.

They persist. They demand attention. You cannot ignore them. Someone must remember how they suffered and how they died.

Many police officers leave the areas they love after retirement. Mountain cops move to the coast, coastal cops move inland. Some people wonder why they do this. Other cops understand, though. You cannot banish ghosts; you can only leave them behind.

18

Tush-hogs and Dinosaurs

*T*ush—pronounced with the "uh" sound, not the "yoo" sound—is colloquial southern English for the word that other parts of the world know as *tusk*. A "tush-hog," then, is a large male hog—or boar—with large "tushes" growing out of its mouth. To be proper, one would call it a "tusk-hog"—anywhere but in the South. Here it is an ordinary tush-hog.

The boar is noted for its ugly disposition and its willingness to fight anything that walks, crawls, flies, or slithers. Tush-hogs have been known to kill and eat copperheads and rattlesnakes, even after the snake had first bite. A snake bite will cause the hog's nose to swell a little, but not much else.

All hogs are crafty. You will never keep a hog penned once it learns about freedom. They are also prolific breeders that have been able to crowd in on the bear population in the Great Smoky Mountains. Hogs are survivalists.

Tush-hog is a term used to identify honky-tonk brawlers who share the attributes of their namesake. Most were gone from Clinton Highway before I hit the streets, but a few were still around. They had been done in by two things—increased law enforcement and a new generation of highway denizens. The new Clinton Highway drinkers did not brawl with fists and bottles. They would shoot or cut at the drop of a hat, but they never learned the old rules.

You did not have to be big to be a tush-hog, but most of them were. The authentic tush-hog prided himself on being able to batter his opponent to the ground with brute force. Of course, they occasionally employed a pool cue or beer bottle.

My first encounter with a genuine tush-hog came when I had only been on the streets a short while. I was dispatched to what was then a topless bar up near the Anderson County line. Inside I found a man—a mountain of a man—with salt-and-pepper hair and beard. He had the battered look of an old prizefighter. Several people were crouching behind the bar as the tush-hog hurled everything he could get his hands on at them.

"That's enough!" I said loudly. I would have called for backup, but none was available at the moment.

He turned and looked at me through bleary eyes as if trying to focus. Reeling, he took two steps in my direction, then stopped. "Look," he said to the people behind the bar, "the Sheriff's Department is hiring midgets."

"Put your hands on the bar and spread your legs," I told him. "You're under arrest for being drunk and disorderly." My face was flaming at the remark about midgets, but I strove to remain calm. Making an error with a man his size, I knew, could prove fatal.

"You ain't gonna try to arrest me by yourself, are you?" He staggered again as if unable to believe his eyes.

"I've already arrested you. You just haven't realized it yet. This is the last time I'm going to tell you—put your hands on the bar now!"

"Why you four-eyed little bastard. I'll whip your ass!" First a comment about my stature, then a reference to my eyesight. He staggered toward me, fists raised.

The shock in his eyes was a wonder to behold as I stepped in with my PR 24 side-handled baton and began to wear out his sensitive shins. When properly used, this type of baton moves at forty times the velocity of an ordinary baton. He tried to back pedal, but he was too drunk. He went down like a mighty oak tree.

"Tim-BER!" someone yelled from behind the bar.

"Roll over," I said, "and put your hands behind your back. If you don't, I'll take your head off."

As I was leading my tush-hog from the bar a few minutes later, an old state trooper pulled up and got out of his cruiser "John," my prisoner said to the trooper, almost sobbing, "this little snit almost broke both my legs. Used to be a cop would give you a fair fight. Now they want to *humiliate* you."

"I know," the old trooper said. "The world has changed. Now get in, and don't give the officer any more trouble."

Lighting a cigarette, I watched the old trooper almost gently put my prisoner in the car. "I see you know him."

"Yeah, he's been out here a long time. I'm ready to retire, and he was kickin' ass on this highway when I started. It took five of us to arrest him the first time I ever ran up on him. Of course, that was before them fancy nightsticks you all carry now. It was man-to-man back then." It was apparent that he resented the new tool more than the old tush-hog in my car.

"I guess technology does everyone in," I said, watching the big, lumbering trooper light a stubby cigar between his teeth.

"The breed's dyin', that's for sure. Never thought I'd see Verlin laid low like this. You're Hunter, aren't you?"

"Yes, I am."

"They're talkin' about you on the highway, even over in Anderson County. They call you 'The Headhunter' and 'Mighty Mite,' when they ain't callin' you somethin' worse. The word is you're buckin' for some kind of record."

"I just do my job," I told him. "It's what the county pays me to do."

"Well, whatever." He started for his cruiser. "After what just happened, you shouldn't have any trouble with the rest of the tush-hogs. Verlin has always about been the king out here."

117

"Doesn't really matter," I answered. "When I tell them they're under arrest, I mean it. It's just a matter of what it takes to make the arrest."

"Damn if all you young cops ain't *serious*," the old trooper said.

I never did see the old trooper again. A few months later I heard he had retired and moved to Florida. His word proved prophetic, however. Some months later I was dispatched to another Clinton Highway nightspot. I knew there was a real problem. The owner hated cops as much as anyone I had ever met.

"I've got Rafer White in here causin' problems," the owner said as I got out of the car. "You'd better call for another car."

"I'll talk to him," I said.

"It's Rafer White! Do you know who he is?"

"I've heard of him. Like I said, I'll talk to him."

"It's your funeral." I could tell he was torn between the desire to have me remove Rafer and the hope that Rafer would hurt me.

Rafer White was dancing with a middle-aged female barfly. He had cleared the floor and was dancing a fairly graceful waltz. He swung his partner as the jukebox blared out "Cheatin' Heart."

"Mister White," I said, tapping him on the shoulder. "My name is David Hunter. I want you to step outside so we can talk."

His face clouded for a moment, then he sighed. "Kin I finish this dance before we go?"

"Sure." I leaned against the wall and waited for him.

"Which one of these is your car?" I asked as I was cuffing him outside.

"The old blue Maverick," he answered. He was a tall, powerfully built man. It was easy to see why he could have earned respect in his day.

"You don't have to tow his car," the bar owner said, following us outside. "He can leave it here."

"Nope, I'm responsible for it," I answered, filling out my paperwork.

118

"I don't want a wrecker on the lot. It's bad for business."

"Too bad," I answered, "because there will be one here in about five minutes."

"I know my rights," the bar owner said, walking over and reaching for my cruiser door.

"If you open that door, I'll arrest you for interfering with an officer."

"I ain't afraid of you." He opened the door. "Rafer, if you wanna leave. . . ."

Rafer swung in the seat with remarkable speed and kicked the bar owner in the face. The man hit the ground and sat up, blood streaming from his mouth. "Call the law on me again, you sonofabitch," Rafer said.

The old tush-hog had some fire left after all.

"I'll get a warrant," the bar owner sputtered through a bloody mouth. "You just wait and see!"

"Tell you what," I said, patting the bar owner on the back. "You forget about the assault warrant, and I'll probably forget to charge you with trying to let my prisoner escape."

Rafer and I both chuckled as the bar owner stomped back inside indignantly. He never did charge Rafer, and I charged him only with public drunkenness. He was out with time served in a couple of days.

The old tush-hogs of Clinton Highway were legendary in their day, fighting across two counties. There was a time when an officer could *depend* on a fight when he entered the domain of the tush-hogs. Things have changed, though. Verlin was right. The new breed is different.

The Clinton Highway tush-hog has gone the way of the dinosaur. We will never see their like again.

19

Robin Hood They Ain't

Petty criminals, whether they be burglars, purse snatchers, bad check artists, or even hold-up men, like to portray themselves as romantic figures at war with a cruel society. Literature and films have been only too glad to support this image because it sells. The fact is, these poor deluded people hardly even qualify as "professional criminals." They spend more time behind bars than outside. That they are caught so often tells you something of their expertise. Professionals are seldom encountered by street cops because they do not get caught very often.

Even in this pathetic underworld of inept criminals, some are in a category by themselves. I was lucky enough to watch one of these so-called professionals as he built an airtight case against himself during an arrest for a simple traffic violation. It happened early in my career, and I never forgot it.

He had been arrested by a state trooper on a traffic violation. The trooper was ready to end his shift and did not want to arrest the man, a surly red-headed South Carolinian. He was left with no choice when the suspect refused to sign a citation for driving on an expired tag.

The suspect, short and stocky, came off the elevator at

the jail making comments about "hillbilly cops, with nothing better to do than arrest law-abiding citizens." He sneered and made rude remarks during the entire booking process. When the trooper had finished his arrest report, he slid a sheet across to the suspect.

"Here, sign this."

"What is it?" the suspect asked.

"It's a release for your car. It says I left it at the scene instead of towing it," the trooper told him.

"Well, I ain't signin' nothin'. If you hadn't played supercop, I'd be in Georgia by now."

"Come on," the trooper said, "this is going to cause me problems. I'd like to go home."

"You shoulda thought of that before you hauled me in," the man said with a smile.

The trooper left angrily. The suspect sat smiling a smug smile, certain that he had scored one on a hick cop. I sat down to do my paperwork. Before I could ask the first question, he leaned back with his hands behind his head.

"I ain't answerin' any of your questions, either. Tell me how much my fine is and call me a cab, so I can go back out there and pick up my car."

"Let me explain something to *you*, pal," I told him. "I don't care whether you answer my questions, but you don't get out until I get my information. As for your car, the trooper has gone out to inventory the contents and have it pulled in because you wouldn't sign the release."

"What?" He sat straight up. "He can't inventory my car. The keys are in the bag I gave you when I came in."

"Wrong. I gave them to him when he left. They'll be with the car when you pick it up. Now, are you going to cooperate, or do you want to stay here until you do cooperate?"

"It won't matter," he said, slumping in the chair. "I won't be leaving anyway." He was still sitting with his head down when the smiling trooper returned with the additional warrants. When the trooper opened the trunk, he found two ounces of marijuana, several grams of cocaine, and a set of burglary tools.

Another criminal in Knox County—a young black man of shaky gender—holds a special place in my memory. Most of his adult life has been spent in the pen, where he is very popular. I will call him Carla.

Until the early 1980s Carla's only criminal activity was writing bad checks. He was good at it because it was hard to perceive him as a criminal. Carla, whose real name is extremely masculine, looks for all the world like a little girl dressed in her father's clothes. When he is in drag, he looks like Gladys Knight.

Needing money, Carla decided to knock over a bank in 1980. He was somewhat limited in his options, as he could not drive and had no friends who could. After robbing a bank in downtown Knoxville, Carla decided to make his getaway on a city bus.

Carla made a clean escape, then panicked. He rode the bus two blocks and bailed out, leaving most of the money to be recovered by the police. He had, however, stuffed several hundred dollars into his pocket, caught a cab, and headed for the airport. Fate was conspiring against Carla, though. If he had not taken the cab, he never would have been caught. Carla was the last person the police would have suspected.

It just so happened that the Sheriff's Department was looking for a murderer at the same time. The murderer was five foot ten inches, stocky, about 200 pounds, and was wearing a mustache. Carla was cleanshaven, about 120 pounds, and stood five foot four inches. The cab driver, however, called the Sheriff's Department and told the dispatcher that he had just taken a black man to the airport and that the man was "a dead-ringer" for the murder suspect.

By the time Sheriff's deputies converged on the airport, Carla's description had been broadcast by the city police. They picked him up, and he confessed. Carla was used to being captured.

As an armed bandit, Carla was in the same category as two good ol' boys who were overcome by the munchies one night after spending all their money on pot. They decided to kill two birds with one stone. They entered an all-night hamburger stand armed with a shotgun and demanded all the money and twelve hamburgers to go.

When the clerk explained that at that time of the evening there were no hamburgers prepared, they decided to wait. While they were waiting, someone driving by saw the shot gun and called the police. Upon hearing the sirens, the two fled with the hamburgers but forgot the money.

A few minutes later one of the Knoxville Police Department K-9 units found them hiding under a nearby bridge. Just before being sent to the pen, one of them told me, "What really pisses me off, Hunter, was that the damned dog ate all my hamburgers. I didn't get a single one."

Many criminals are under the influence of intoxicants when they do their deeds. This was the case with a burglar arrested by Mike Upchurch and me one early morning after he had burglarized a small bar.

The place he burglarized was owned by a man who did not want to pay for keeping lights on at night. As a result, it became a favorite place to be broken into by local thieves. It had been entered so often that most of the windows had been replaced by plywood. This led Upchurch to predict that future thieves would have to break the windows with a chain saw.

The owner called one night to have a report made on his latest burglary. After Mike did the report, we looked around for clues, though with little hope. The thief had taken only Budweiser beer and Marlboro cigarettes, which was a little unusual, but offered no real clues. Then, a few feet from the building, we found a cold can of Budweiser.

Moving on toward the road, we found a pack of Marlboros, then another cold Budweiser. Like Hansel and Gretel, we followed a trail of Budweisers and Marlboros across the highway and up into the woods. The trail ended at an abandoned house trailer. On the steps was an empty Budweiser can, still cold. Inside we found a drunk juvenile, passed out in a corner. His field jacket was cinched at the waist. Apparently he was too drunk to know that his loot was falling out as he staggered from the scene of the crime.

When the youth was brought up on burglary charges in juvenile court, the judge sat shaking his head as Upchurch drawled out his story. "This has to be true," the judge said, "no officer would *invent* a story like that."

Early one morning I drove up on a small pickup truck parked by the road. The side window had been broken out, and the radio was dangling from the dash. The hood of the truck was still warm. Puzzled, I looked around. From across the field I saw someone with a flashlight walking toward me. It turned out he was the night watchman for a dairy farm and had left the truck while he made his rounds. A passing thief had seized the opportunity, only to have me drive up before he could escape.

The thief had bolted over a barbed wire fence, cutting his hand in the process. As the watchman walked toward me, the thief was trapped between us. As the watchman's light fell on him, he was lying on his belly with his face buried in what we in the South call "a cow-pile." He was still trying to get it out of his ears and nose when I left him at the jail. Theft is—pardon the pun—a smelly business.

Ask the gasoline thief who sneaked up behind a camper and dropped in his siphon hose. The owner caught him a few minutes later, throwing up and unable to run away. He had sucked up the contents of the portable toilet instead of gasoline.

This next story is from a banker, not a cop, but it deserves telling. The banker is assigned to a branch that is less than prosperous. He was never happy with the assignment and was angry because he felt he was not in a place where he could advance. He even had trouble with his parking spot. Patrons of a bar across the street tended to use his space and were not at all impressed by the sign that read "Branch Manager."

One afternoon he returned from lunch in a particularly bad mood, only to find an old car parked in his space. A young girl sat behind the wheel; the engine was idling. Filled with righteous indignation, he jumped from his car.

"All right," he yelled, "get that car out of my space! *Do it right now!*"

The girl glanced in the rearview mirror, threw the car in gear, and screeched off the lot. He stood there, both pleased and surprised. Generally people in that section of town had not been overly impressed with bank managers.

As he stood there enjoying his triumph, a man ran out of the bank wearing a ski mask and holding a pistol in one hand and an open money bag in the other. He screeched to a halt at the empty parking space, then ran down the alley, money flying from the bag. The police picked him up a few blocks away, still wearing the ski mask.

The most daring desperado I ever met, though, may be a legless paint sniffer who was one of my wards when I worked in the jail. He had lost his legs while lying intoxicated one night across a railroad track.

When I encountered him at the jail, he was awaiting trial for burglarizing the same hardware store twice. Both times the manager had found the paint sniffer passed out when the store opened in the morning. Both times he was covered with silver paint. The mode of intoxication is to spray the paint into a bag and put it over the face. Paint sniffers do not use anything else. It is quick, cheap, and eventually lethal.

I was curious, though, as to why he kept burglarizing the same place. He was quick to explain. "It's the only place I can get to since I lost my legs, so I do the best I can. I'm a handicapped thief, Hunter, but I ain't *crippled*. I hate people who whine. As long as I can practice my trade at all, I'm gonna *do* it."

The list could go on. There was the attempted rapist, who not only was impotent, but left his checkbook on the intended victim's couch. I will not forget the out-of-town thief who was being chased by the police on a foggy night. Stopping on a bridge, he jumped over the railing, thinking he was at ground level. He was forty feet in the air.

Every cop has his favorite "stupid criminal" story. One thing is certain, though. Robin Hood they ain't.

20

My Strength Is as
That of Ten

Cops, particularly southern cops raised in the tradition of chivalry, believe they will always win their battles. Logic tells them differently, and experience tells them differently, but they persist in believing their "strength is as that of ten, because their hearts are pure." This belief makes it possible for them to go out into a hostile world—where they are always outnumbered and at the mercy of anyone who decides to take them by surprise—and enforce the law.

They do not persist in believing this because they are stupid. To the contrary, most present-day southern cops are very bright people. This is insured by the process of elimination. There are always more people who want to be cops than there are openings. Before putting on a badge at the Knox County Sheriff's Department, an officer has passed a written test, a psychiatric evaluation, a rigid background check, and an oral interview with a civilian board. More importantly, the officer has spent a couple of years as a jailer handling very dangerous prisoners.

The badge means something. The officer wearing it has earned it. The officer is bright, honest, and physically and emotionally tough. Still they believe—deep in their innermost beings—that the good guys always win. It is a self-defense mechanism. Cops believe this for the same reason that a lion tamer believes that the beasts will not turn and rip him apart; for the same reason a tightrope walker believes he will not lose his balance.

You *have* to believe, or you cannot do the job.

Some things reinforce a cop's confidence that he can do the job. Cops wear a symbol of authority on their chest. It is ingrained in society's collective mind that a badge is to be obeyed. A cop *expects* obedience and leaves no doubt that he expects it. It is a potent, but not foolproof, combination, especially in the rural South.

Self-confidence can go too far. When this happens to a cop, it is called "tombstone courage" because a tombstone is what it will get you.

A cop acquires a reputation when he spends a lot of time on the streets. A good reputation as a tough, fair officer is the result of hard, consistent work. Sometimes a little luck gives you a boost, as I discovered early in my days as a patrol officer. Some stories also tend to grow with the telling. Houdini learned this, too. Very often in his career he received credit for escapes he never performed. When this occurs, you just keep quiet and "let on like you done it."

My first such incident happened when I had been on the streets a very short time. I pulled up to a red light on Clinton Highway behind a Harley-Davidson motorcycle. The rider belonged to a small-time gang that aspired to being a group of real "outlaws." At the time, though, I could not tell one biker from another.

Apparently the rider was not aware of my presence. When the light changed, he did a "wheelie," screeching away with the motorcycle standing on the rear wheel. Doing this in front of a cop is like spitting on him. Righteous indignation seized me as I hit the blue lights and siren.

He glanced into his rearview mirror and gunned the engine. I called for a backup unit as we screamed north on Clinton Highway. Just south of the Anderson County line, the biker skidded onto a gravel lot, jumped from the bike and sprinted toward a run-down building with me in close foot pursuit.

He went through the door, and someone tried to slam it in my face. Knowing that I would never be able to get him if they locked me out, I kicked the flimsy door open, bringing a scream of outrage from the person behind it, and pushed my way in.

I found myself inside a relatively small room, with peeling walls, a pool table, a juke box, a wet bar, and about eighteen bikers and assorted women. The biker I had been chasing turned to face me, smiling wickedly. He was a modern barbarian, replete with chains and leather. A gold tooth only added to his leering smile. The rest of the crowd closed around me, smelling of stale beer and unwashed bodies.

Events seemed to move in slow motion. My backup might have been seconds away, or minutes. Television cops would have had a humorous quip to break the silence, but humor evaded me at the moment. So I did the only thing I could think of.

"You're under arrest. Walk outside and put your hands on the side of my car," I told him.

"You've got guts for such a little man," he said. He was still smiling arrogantly, but I detected just the slightest bit of doubt deep in his bloodshot eyes. At five-feet, six inches, I was not the *shortest* Knox County Officer, and at 185 pounds I was not the *smallest;* but I was looking up at everyone in the room.

"Right now I've got you for reckless driving, driving under the influence, and fleeing to avoid arrest. If I hear another remark about my physical attributes, I'm going to add disorderly conduct," I said.

"What makes you think I'm going *anywhere* with you, to be charged with *anything*?" He sounded angry, but now the doubt in his eyes was distinct.

"You'll do it, unless you're stupid as well as drunk. There are cops coming from all over the county. They know where I am, and they have your tag number. So get outside, now!" I patted my holster meaningfully, perfectly aware that I would not even be able to hold onto the weapon if the crowd decided to take me down.

He stood, turning it over in his mind. The crowd was muttering. At the time I was unaware that the man I was arresting—I will call him Weasel—was the vice-president of the club. A word from him and everyone would have tap-danced on my head.

"All right," he said, turning on his heel, "I ain't goin' to jail for killin' a cop." Following him outside, I allowed myself to breathe normally again, thankful that my voice had held. I became aware of just how hard my heart was pounding as I told the dispatcher to cancel my backup, or at least slow them down.

When backup arrived a few minutes later, I was doing the paperwork. My car was surrounded by bikers looking in the window.

"Everything all right?" the sergeant asked.

"Just fine, Sergeant. I appreciate the help, but everything's under control now. This gentleman decided to cooperate." I saw another unit pull on the lot. The sergeant waved him off as he left.

"I've sent my people away," I said. "Send yours away."

He stared at me in the rearview mirror, then signaled the bikers to go back inside. He was moving around in the seat, as if trying to make himself comfortable.

"Hand me the dope you just dropped behind the seat," I said, "and anything else you're carrying. Give it to me now, and I may or may not charge you with it, depending on how much you've got."

"What dope?"

"Don't play games. I check behind that seat every time I arrest someone. Hand it to me!" I had not seen him drop the dope, but I knew he had done it. With a sigh, he reached behind the seat and handed me a baggie with two joints in it.

"Am I charged?"

"Not for two joints. Is that all?"

"That's all," he said. "What are my charges again?"

"Just driving under the influence," I answered.

"What about the other charges. You just bluffing?"

"I never bluff, but I think a man deserves a reward for not being stupid. Someone could have gotten seriously hurt back there," I said.

"Would you have used that gun?" he asked.

"What do you think?"

"I'm under arrest, ain't I?" he said with a chuckle.

It was a minor incident in a patrol career, but it had repercussions. One of the backup officers put out the word that I was a "hot-dog," just full of "tombstone courage." More importantly, Weasel put out the word on the highway, "The little bastard is crazy, but he's fair." That is not a bad reputation for an officer on Clinton Highway to have, or anywhere else for that matter.

It paid dividends a year later.

Chuck Pittman had arrested a woman on Clinton Highway for driving under the influence. I administered the test and was doing my paperwork as Chuck headed in.

"A 10-59 in progress at the city limits!" I heard Pittman yell. "Male subject is assaulting female subject."

I threw my cruiser into gear and went to assist him. Another cruiser rolled in just ahead of me. The biker, who had been beating his wife, fled inside the bar when he saw us coming. Inside we found several bikers and their wives, or old ladies, as they call them. These were not minor-league bikers, but full-fledged outlaws. They sat still, however, as we dragged out the assailant. They knew he could be bailed out and would not hassle with the law over such a minor thing.

As we were loading the biker into the second cruiser, Pittman made a discovery. "My prisoner's gone!"

In the excitement, Chuck had forgotten to lock the front door of his cruiser. Apparently the woman who had been assaulted had opened the door and let the first woman out.

"I don't believe it," Pittman moaned, "that woman is handcuffed. It's below zero out here. She'll be a *popsicle* by morning."

"Come on, Chuck, she probably left with the woman

131

who let her out," I said. I knew how he felt, though. The idea of a prisoner freezing with *your* handcuffs on is frightening.

The next night I paid a visit to my old friend Weasel. The door opened a crack, and I saw his bearded face on the other side.

"Aren't you gonna kick the door in tonight, Hunter?"

"You don't even have to talk to me, but I'd appreciate it," I said.

"Come into my office," he said, opening the door. There were three or four others inside. They muttered but said nothing out loud.

"What can I do for you?" Weasel asked, sitting down at a table and picking up a can of Millers.

"We had an incident up the highway last night."

"I heard, but none of my people were involved," he said.

"I know that, but I thought you might be able to get word to the people who *were* involved."

"I might be able to," he said, drinking the contents of the can in a long swallow. "I just might be able to do that, Hunter."

"If you should see them, just tell them that Pittman is a friend of mine and that I resent his embarrassment. I want the girl delivered to roll call no later than Friday. Also, we need the cuffs back. If this doesn't happen, tell them I'm going to develop an overwhelming interest in motorcycles. There are about twenty *legal* reasons to stop a bike. You might tell them I always keep my word."

"I'll tell them," he said, "but this ain't altar boys we're talkin' about. They're outlaws."

"I know, but do it for me anyway."

I was the only officer at roll call Friday who was not shocked when the bearded biker knocked on the door and politely asked for Officer Pittman. The biker stood, leather cap in hand. "Officer, we got your prisoner out in the car. She'll be pleadin' guilty to drunk drivin'. Your cuffs got lost, but me and the others took up a collection and bought you these." It was a brand new set of Peerless cuffs.

They would not have given up a "brother" or even a prized "old lady," but I had banked on the woman being a "momma," not worth the hassle she had caused. I knew a biker's priorities and banked on them. Sometimes things work out.

So it goes. It is not always *reality* that counts, to paraphrase Oscar Wilde, but what people *think* is real. Reputation is worth a lot to a cop, along with a lot of hard work.

21

Why Are They Saying Mean Things About Me?

The hardest thing for a rookie cop to understand is the people who hate him for no apparent reason. These people constitute a very small minority, but their hatred is such a visible thing that at times they seem to be in the large majority.

Most rookies are so proud of their new uniforms that they look for excuses to wear them. They will pick up their wives on the way home and "drop in" for dinner at a familiar place. They strut like roosters, wearing the uniform they have worked so hard to earn.

The rookie quickly finds that this is not a good idea. There are always people watching who will call in and say that they have seen a cop "running around with women, on duty." It is easier to avoid a problem than to explain.

Aside from the complaints, there are crazies out there who would like nothing better than to provoke a violent confrontation. Officers do not want their families involved in such situations, and they soon learn that the uniform they respect so much is like a red flag to many civilians who—for whatever reason—hate cops.

Another problem crops up when an officer tries to eat in uniform, even on duty. There is *always* someone with a grievance to be aired. If the officer refuses to listen, no matter how politely, he will be reported as rude and arrogant. If he listens to every complaint, he will never finish a meal while it is warm enough to enjoy. Officers learn to pick up their food to go so they can hide behind a building somewhere and eat in peace. This limits the menu, but is more comfortable in the long run.

My first brush with irrational hatred came when I was still a reserve officer. I was sent to a hospital one Saturday morning to guard a prisoner in the intensive care unit. There was little danger he would try to escape, but prisoners are not guarded for that reason only. Some prisoners have violent enemies who would love to find them helpless.

I relieved the officer on duty at a quarter to seven. He was sitting at the nurses' station where he could watch the aging black man he was assigned to guard. He briefed me before leaving.

"The nurses have been really nice. They kept my coffee cup filled all night, and when you need a break, hospital security comes up to relieve you."

I took out a paperback and settled in for a long eight hours. There was a chair at the back of the office where I could watch my prisoner out of sight of the patients. A couple of minutes later I became aware of a large black woman in a nurse's uniform standing in front of me with her hands on her hips. She was breathing deeply, obviously enraged.

"I am the *head nurse* on this ward, and I want you out of here. Right now!"

"I am a *police officer*," I replied, "assigned to guard a prisoner. I just relieved an officer who was here all night without problems."

"If the night shift wants to let the storm troopers upset their patients, I can't stop it. But we don't need guns in here to guard one sick old man who couldn't leave if he wanted to. I won't have you disturbing my patients."

"I'm here to *protect* that man," I replied, "and your patients can't even *see* me. What's the real problem?" There were several nurses behind her, both black and white.

They appeared embarrassed.

"You may think you're God out there on the streets," she was almost screaming, "but I'm in charge here. Now get out of this ward!"

"I'm going to check for outside doors. If there aren't any, I'll go outside the swinging doors. I do have an assignment, however, and I *will* carry it out."

Finding no other entrances, I went outside and took up a post where I could still see my prisoner through the glass. In a moment the nurse was outside, angrier than ever.

"I want you away from this door, now! This is a hospital, not a prison!" The bile was dripping from her voice, and hatred filled her eyes. My patience had run out.

"Let me explain something to you, *nurse*. You have been extremely rude, which will be reported to your supervisor. I have been polite, but my patience is at an end. It is against the law to interfere with a police officer in the line of duty. Now get away from me before I charge you with disorderly conduct."

She stormed away, her fat buttocks twitching in an indignant manner. A few minutes later she returned with a puzzled security officer. "I want him out of here right now!" she said, pointing at me.

"He's *supposed* to be here," the security officer said. "He can go stand by the bed if he wants to. My apologies," he said, turning toward me. "I'll check and let you have a break whenever you're ready."

"We'll get this straightened out at the staff meeting," she said. "I might have known that all you storm troopers would stick together. You all have the same mentality!"

It was my first encounter with a cop-hater, but not the last.

Every neighborhood has a resident cop-hater whose self-appointed task is to make certain that officers do not waste the taxpayers' money. Unfortunately, they only see what they want to see.

"I want you to know that this is disgraceful, and I'm going to call the sheriff," the man told me. He was about fifty, well dressed, and seemingly rational, except where cops are concerned.

"What's disgraceful?" I asked, taking the lid off my coffee. I was on my way to work after a three-day break.

"Your cruiser was parked here at six yesterday evening. It hasn't moved since then." He was livid.

"You're saying I've been here thirteen hours?"

"I can't think of a better explanation, can *you*?"

"Yes, I can. This is the junction of an interstate highway, heavily patrolled. Officers stop here for coffee quite often. I would suggest that you saw another cruiser here last night. Mine has been parked in my driveway for three days."

"I figured you'd have some kind of excuse. I'm calling the sheriff, anyway." I did not argue. He would believe what he wanted to believe.

Not long ago in Dallas, Texas, a patrol officer stopped a car to write a citation. As he was writing the citation, an individual approached him and provoked an argument. During the following scuffle, the suspect took the officer's weapon. As the officer pleaded with the man, the crowd around them began to chant, "Shoot him. Shoot him." When he shot the officer, the crowd chanted, "Shoot him again."

Such incidents chill officers to the bone. Feeling already isolated and under attack, they wonder if it will happen to them next—and why. The man in Dallas had previously assaulted another officer. He hated cops.

In Knox County there is almost one hundred percent chance that a patrol officer will be assaulted in any given year. The assaults will range from minor to serious, but they will happen. No one else gets excited about it.

"This guy wants to make a deal," the assistant attorney general said. "He'll plead guilty to drunk driving if we'll drop the assault charges."

"Why drop them?" I asked. "We have witnesses. He's guilty of assaulting two officers."

"Did anybody bleed? Any broken bones?"

"No, but we had abrasions and bruises. One of the officers had a shirt ripped off."

"We'll stipulate that he has to pay for the shirt, but we're dropping the assault charges to avoid going to criminal court. It's your job to fight with violent people. It's an occupational hazard."

The assistant attorney general was right. After a while, officers stop filing assault and battery warrants. It is pointless. I do not know how many times I have been assaulted through the years, but I know how many people I have convicted of assaulting me—one. That one was part of a plea bargain, or I would not have gotten it.

A cop's most horrible nightmare, though, is not physical assault but the fear that he will be crucified in the press.

A recent headline said something to this effect: "Parents Allege That Officers Beat Crippled Son." The newspapers went on for days, telling the family's story in graphic language. Much was made of the fact that the officers did not come forward to defend themselves. Nothing was said about the fact that an internal affairs investigation was in progress and that officers are constrained to await the results of an investigation before commenting publicly.

According to the family, the police were called to take away a drunken family member. The officers allegedly went berserk and began to beat the intoxicated man. The "crippled" brother allegedly came to the rescue and was brutalized. The "crippled" man was allegedly suffering from a neurological disorder.

A few weeks later the facts emerged. Officers had also been injured in the free-for-all. The hospital where the "cripple" had been treated told the investigators that they had definitely proved that the man had no neurological disorder. A check of police records revealed that both the "cripple" and his brother had been charged with similar crimes in the past.

This story appeared on the back pages. There was no headline on the front page to proclaim "Family Lied, Officers Cleared." It is not front page news when an officer is found to be innocent. Later, when the two men were indicted by a grand jury that had *all* the facts at their disposal, a few lines acknowledged the fact.

As an aside, one mayoral candidate demanded that all officers involved in the incident be fired without a hearing. He later asked the police department to support him in his bid for the office and was offended when they chose not to do so.

Why are they saying those mean things about me? I am not certain of all the reasons, but I can pinpoint two. First, some people hate *all* forms of authority. The police officer is merely a focus of authority—especially in the South where rugged individualism is raised almost to a holy level.

Second, there *have* been abuses of power by police officers. They are few, but they happen. Of the thousands of excessive force charges filed against officers every year, very few turn out to be true. Most complaints are filed by disgruntled persons who are seeking revenge.

The very term *excessive force* angers some officers. "What the hell does it mean?" one officer asked me. "If the guy comes at me with a tire tool and I break his arm with my baton, that's all right. If I misjudge and fracture his skull, that's excessive. I didn't hit his head any harder than his arm. How do you measure force?"

The officer is right. There is no scale to measure "sufficient force" or "excessive force." I recently spent a frustrating fifteen minutes along with two other officers attempting to cuff and load an abusive drunk. He cursed and abused us the entire time. We could have subdued him in moments had we not been afraid to do what we were trained to do—use the baton on vulnerable areas until the prisoner complies. Instead, we skinned ourselves up and looked ridiculous because we have become so afraid of "excessive force" complaints.

The only truly "nonlethal weapon" invented in this century is denied most officers, not because it is dangerous, but because it reminds people of the cattle prods used against demonstrators during the sixties. It brings a scream from libertarians and civil rights lawyers.

The "stun gun," available in sizes small enough to be worn on the belt, delivers a jolt of electricity that will make the most violent prisoner comply. It ends the need for wrestling and pounding with sticks. It delivers a lot of voltage, but almost no amps (which cause the damage from electrical shock). The shock is disabling, but it does no physical damage, except for a small brown spot when applied to bare skin.

Most of the time it is not necesary to use the stun gun. You merely hold it up and touch the button. The prisoner *sees* the sparks and calms down. I once acted as a volunteer in a demonstration. After one touch of the electrodes, all I wanted to do was stay away from it.

Stun guns became popular in the mid-eighties, but they were banned by most departments because of public relations problems. "We can't shock 'em," one officer said. "I guess I'll go back to the *humane* way and beat them with a stick."

In other words, even though appropriate technology is available, modern cops are still using methods used by the ancient Romans.

Why are they saying all those mean things about me? This question is especially important to a person who sees himself as a knight in shining armor, a good guy, Mr. Clean. There is a touch of the romantic, especially in southern cops. It injures the self-image to be hated for the very things he is so proud of. Deep in his inner being, he is not a cop so much as Galahad looking for a damsel in distress.

22

Damned If You Do, Damned If You Don't

The white Chevrolet wandered back and forth across the center line of 25W, northbound. The driver was drunk, of that I had no doubt. It was a classic pattern, just like the films at the police academy.

It was not the intoxication of the driver that caused my heart to pound, however, but the car itself. A few weeks earlier, a Knox County officer had been gunned down in a secluded park in North Knox County, a few miles away. The officer's description: A beat-up, white Chevrolet, 1965 to 1967 model, just like the one ahead of me, driven by a shaggy, bearded, white male. The shaggy driver had drawn a weapon upon approach and had shot the officer while the passenger hunkered down out of view.

As I pulled in closer to look at the Chevrolet, the passenger turned and saw my vehicle, then immediately slid down out of sight. The driver, with long, shaggy hair, began to watch me in his rearview mirror. I radioed a description of the vehicle and my position, took a deep breath, then hit the blue lights.

The driver immediately accelerated. I could hear his carburetor cut in as he pulled away. It was an electrifying and horrible moment. I was a rookie patrolman and had never

143

been in hot pursuit. All my knowledge was theoretical; the situation was real. To chase, or not to chase, was the question.

Pursuits are a nightmare, both for officers in the field and police administrators. It is a no-win situation. You cannot issue an order forbidding pursuits. If you do this, criminals will *never* stop. On the other hand, if a pursued vehicle crashes into an innocent party, the officer and department may be found liable. Damned if you do, damned if you don't, is the fatalistic attitude of most cops.

"I'm in pursuit," I told the dispatcher, who immediately cleared the channel.

In the movies we watch with bated breath as police cars hurtle down crowded streets, mowing down mailboxes and other obstacles. We watch it begin, then we watch it end in a flaming wreck and a crescendo of music. A real pursuit is a surrealistic nightmare. *Will I make it through the next intersection? Will a car drive out of a side road?*

It had been raining that night. I watched in silent terror as the speedometer climbed to ninety, realizing that a touch of the brakes would send me sliding into eternity. We were approaching a four-way-stop intersection. Even in the early morning hours there is traffic on 25W.

We hurtled through the intersection, my blue lights flashing and my siren wailing. Immediately, I began to think of the stretch of road ahead. It was typical East Tennessee road—up and down, a series of long, curving turns, at that time slick with rain. I was convinced, though, that I had a potential cop killer ahead.

"I'm leaving the county," I said, "notify Anderson County." Other Knox County officers were en route to assist. I had heard them—without really listening—intent on controlling the vehicle through the curves.

We climbed, then dropped off toward a straightaway, long for East Tennessee. In reality, the stretch of straight road was about a quarter of a mile.

His speed began to drop off. Eighty, seventy, sixty, then fifty. For a moment, I thought he was going to stop. He braked sharply, then turned left, attempting to head down a side road. Sliding sideways and attempting to maintain control, I heard his engine stall, then die, the front of his vehicle coming to rest in the opposite direction.

Rolling out of my vehicle, I racked a round into my shotgun and aimed at the driver. I could hear his engine turn over, then catch and start. The temptation to put twelve pellets of double ought buckshot through the driver's side window was almost overwhelming. I wanted it to end. Training overcame my impulse, however. I jumped back into my cruiser.

"We're southbound," I told the dispatcher, "running at approximately seventy miles per hour, approaching Knox County."

I heard my lieutenant's voice crackle over the airways. He was driving toward me, coming northbound. Without warning, the driver of the Chevrolet drifted into the northbound lane as we entered the long curve again. I grabbed the mike to warn the lieutenant that he was meeting a vehicle that was driving in the wrong lane.

To my horror, the engine of my cruiser momentarily stalled. The radio, blue lights, and siren went dead. I was never able to find out why. The best guess was an overheated circuit somewhere in the system.

I breathed a sigh of relief as the lieutenant came around the curve. He was running in the inside lane of the double lane highway. The speeding vehicles missed each other. I saw the lieutenant slide around behind me, just as my equipment came back on. The white Chevrolet drifted back into the southbound lane.

At the first intersection in Knox County, a sheriff's department cruiser entered the chase, getting between me and the suspect vehicle. I lost ground every time my engine stalled out. Moments later, the lieutenant drove around me. By that time, I was running third in my own pursuit.

As we passed the city limits of Knoxville, a police department cruiser entered the chase, then another. It seemed that every time we passed a side street, another city officer joined in.

My engine stalled again at a major intersection. For a moment, I thought I was out of the pursuit. Frustration and rage boiled inside me; then my car started again. I caught up with the pursuit, just as the white Chevrolet took the I-640 exit, westbound. He went east on I-40. Miraculously, no vehicle was hit on the interstate as we wove in and out of traffic.

The white Chevrolet took the business loop at the downtown Knoxville exit, taking us right into the heart of the city. We drove between buildings on mostly deserted streets, the sound of the sirens bouncing eerily from the walls.

Finally exiting on Chapman Highway, he turned south, where we later found that he lived. A few blocks away, he crashed into a city police cruiser that was about to enter the pursuit. Police cars converged. The driver of the white Chevrolet put his car in reverse and backed into a sheriff's department cruiser.

As the two occupants came out fighting, I was more convinced than ever that I had the suspects who had shot a county officer. It was a bad move for them. It is not a good idea to take on fifteen cops with their adrenalin flowing. The fight did not last long.

With the suspects in my back seat, police cars suddenly vanished, going back to wherever they were supposed to be. Knox County pursuit policy is plain and direct. There will be no more than two units involved in a pursuit.

In a matter of minutes I knew that the two prisoners in my car had not shot the police officer. They had been in jail at the time of the shooting. I was amazed. Why had the driver risked his life and mine over traffic violations?

"I didn't wanna go to jail," the driver said with a shrug. "I was drunk and didn't have a driver's license."

Through the years I would cease to be amazed by people willing to risk their lives to avoid an overnight stay in jail. A few years later, along the same stretch of highway I had a suspect push his twelve-year-old daughter out of his car into the path of my cruiser to avoid capture.

The pursuit had started over a broken taillight lens. It covered twelve miles, driven at an average speed of sixty-two miles per hour, and ended in another county. The man thought I had recognized him and was going to arrest him for driving without a license.

The first chase of my career was over. It was also the first time the press ever called me for an interview. I was talking freely when it dawned on me that my bosses would be reading about a pursuit in which fifteen cruisers were involved in a high speed chase. I tried to repair the damage, but with little success.

The bold heading of my first newspaper write-up said, "Fifteen Cruisers Involved in Chase." The reporter ended the story by writing "Though the chase involved speeds of ninety miles an hour, Officer David Hunter stressed that he was extremely cautious because of the wet roads."

An officer has to be cautious.

23

Bloodthirsty Cops, Their Killer Ways

Whenever a civilian is shot by police officers, it is a matter of public concern, and rightly so. Men and women who carry weapons should be monitored closely. Going armed is an awesome responsibility. There are those, however, who try to convey the image of blood-thirsty, killer cops gleefully waiting for the moment when they can kill someone. The facts dispute this image.

At the Knox County Sheriff's Department, at this time there are roughly 125 gun-carrying officers who make regular contact with the public. They are patrol officers, detectives, and warrants officers. About forty more carry guns, but as transportation officers and jail supervisors they would not generally expect to be involved in violent confrontations on the street.

Between January of 1981 and January of 1988, six Knox County officers were shot, one fatally. This is 4.8 percent, or roughly one in twenty of the officers who are on the streets. If the New York Police Department has 28,000 officers, to equal the same percentage of officers shot as Knox County they would have had 1,400 officers shot in the line of duty. Needless to say, this has not happened in New York; had it, it would have caused national concern. In the South, however, this figure raises no eyebrows. The

149

numbers are small by location, and shootings seem almost routine.

I use these statistics only to illustrate a point. During this period when Knox County Deputies were shot at a rate of nearly one in twenty, *not a single civilian was shot by a Knox County officer.* This only takes into account the officers who were actually shot, it does not include those who were merely *shot at.*

Knox County officers are quick to tell you that if they were inclined to be trigger-happy, there is no lack of opportunity. Southern cops chuckle when they hear their counterparts in the North claim that cops often go a whole career without drawing a weapon. A southern street cop who has never drawn a weapon has been hiding under his bed. The reason no civilians were shot for an eight-year period is because Knox County officers practice professional restraint, often to the point of endangering themselves.

Any southern cop can relate stories of incidents where shootings would have not only been justified, but were called for by "the book." Weapons are a fact of life in the laid-back South. The months when you do not draw your weapon are the unusual ones.

One such incident happened to me in 1985. Fire department paramedics called for a cruiser at an apartment complex in north Knox County. Details were sketchy, as they usually are. I knew only that an attempted suicide had barricaded himself inside an apartment. Upon arrival, seeing the firemen crouched behind their truck, I immediately had the dispatcher clear the channel for emergency traffic. Running in a crouch to the fire engine, I asked the paramedics what was going on. A large crowd stood back about 100 yards from the engine.

"We've got a crazy in there," the paramedic said, "and he's armed. He's also slashed himself, but I don't know how badly. When we went through the door, he pointed a weapon at us. I didn't ask questions. I just got the hell out of there. His family says he's violent and dangerous, that he keeps an arsenal at times."

I called for a backup and talked to the man's family.

They said lately he had been fantasizing about being a mercenary soldier and that he had spent much of his adult life in psychiatric wards. I had them sketch the layout of the apartment for me, including the location of all windows.

When my captain arrived to back me up, I filled him in on the details. An insane man, possibly armed with an automatic weapon, bleeding and barricaded inside. "Let's check it out," the captain said. "He may be bleeding to death."

We moved along the building, watching the windows outlined for me by the tenants. Suddenly we walked directly in front of a balcony inset into the wall that the family had not mentioned. Before we could react, the double doors were kicked open from the inside. Our suspect stepped through the door, dropped into a shooting crouch, and pointed a weapon at us.

In a situation like this in the movies, one of the officers would shoot the suspect in the arm, proving that the people who write scripts have never had a weapon pointed at them. The captain and I, both under instant adrenalin surges, dashed for cover. Nearby was a small inset where two walls joined. It was just big enough for me to squeeze into. The captain, who is built like me—short and stocky—continued down the side of the building at a fast clip.

Less than two feet from me the suspect was screaming out obscenities and curses while waving his weapon at the crowd. From my vantage point it appeared to be a semi-automatic, possibly a Colt .45. If he came over the balcony railing I would have to shoot, and I suddenly wondered if my ammunition would take him out before he got off a shot at me. I remembered seeing a picture of a suspect with a dozen rounds in him who had managed to kill a police officer.

I toyed with the idea of knocking the weapon from his hand with my baton, but not for long. If I swung down at the suspect's arm and missed, I realized the momentum probably would make me vulnerable to being shot in the head, or at the very least I would give away my position.

"Drop the weapon or we'll shoot!" The captain had

151

worked his way behind a car in front of the suspect, about thirty yards away.

"Go to hell! I hung heads on poles in Angola. No hick cop is gonna tell me what to do."

Swallowing hard and attempting to bring my breathing under control, I eased around enough so that I could see the suspect. I had passed the point of talking. The man could not be allowed to open fire. There were too many civilians and houses around. Placing my weapon hand against the building, I centered in on his chest and began to squeeze the trigger.

"This is your last warning," the captain yelled. "Drop it, or we'll shoot."

I paused, deciding to give the man one last chance to live. For a split second his life hung in the balance as the hammer of my Smith & Wesson hovered. He dropped the weapon.

I charged in, kicking the weapon away, and attempted to grab him by the belt. Hampered by the weapon in my hand, I was unable to catch him. He ran back inside, slamming the door. I could hear him screaming and cursing inside.

Scooping up the pistol, I took cover again. The weapon was a piston-powered airgun made to look like a real automatic pistol. I breathed a sigh of relief, even though the situation had not ended. At least I had not killed a man holding only an airgun in his hand, although I would have been fully justified, in these circumstances.

By this time other cars had arrived. We covered all the doors and windows as Lieutenant Jim Brackett knocked out a window with my aluminum baton. Dropping his gunbelt, Brackett entered the window, followed by the captain. A moment later, there was screaming from inside, and the captain opened the front door. Five of us rushed in.

At the back of the kitchen the suspect stood, a blond man of thirty or so. He was bleeding from several superficial cuts and was holding a kitchen knife in his hand. "Get out, or I'll kill every one of you!"

"Drop the knife," someone said, "or die. Do it now."

I do not know who spoke, but it was obvious that the scene was about to end, one way or another. The voice carried the finality of authority. The man dropped his weapon, and six officers holstered theirs. We were all over him immediately, finally hobbling him with plastic cuffs. After transporting him to a hospital, we decided not to file charges. It would have been pointless.

When things had cooled off, I spoke to the captain. "We should have killed him," I said. "By the book, we should have killed him."

The captain did not answer but nodded his head, as if considering the matter for the first time.

"I'm glad we didn't, but we *should* have. Both of us endangered ourselves," I said.

Killing another human being is a horrible thing to contemplate. Every cop lives with that specter every time he straps on a weapon. In the simplest terms, we are empowered by the state to use lethal force to protect ourselves and others. When and how we use it is strictly in our hands. There are no judges or politicians on the streets. It speaks highly of police officers that they so seldom invoke that awesome power.

A large number of officers killed in the line of duty die with weapons still holstered. A big percentage of them die in Dixieland, where the accents are soft and the people are friendly.

Bloodthirsty cops with killer ways? The evidence does not bear it out. To the contrary, at the Knox County Sheriff's Department, for the last seven years the score stands: Bad guys 6, Good guys 0.

24

Are Cop Shows Really Real?

Civilians always get around to asking, "Are cop shows *really* real? Are they authentic?"

The answer, of course, is "yes" and "no." It all depends on which show you are talking about. Some are extremely authentic, some leave police officers rolling around on the floor, laughing hysterically, even when the show is a drama. Most police shows are somewhere between the truth and fantasy. In my opinion, "Hill Street Blues" came pretty close to being realistic.

"Hill Street Blues" had a wide range of personalities. Cops were shown as neither saints nor sinners, Boy Scouts or monsters. Early morning roll call was the most realistic part of the show. You always saw a group of sleepy, cynical cops wisecracking and drinking their morning coffee. Even at that, there were things that did not quite ring true.

We always saw the sergeant handing out assignments. That is fine—for patrol officers. You do not, however, announce undercover assignments in roll call. Not that you do not trust your brother officers, but because you know what big mouths they are. Twenty minutes after roll call, most officers will be somewhere eating breakfast and discussing everything that happened at roll call. Not all of them are discreet. An undercover operation announced to thirty people might as well be put on the morning news.

There was also the matter of uniforms. "Hill Street" officers wore cowboy hats and boots, vests, and other paraphernalia with their uniforms. Some wore long sleeves and ties, while others were in short sleeves. Plainclothes officers get away with this. Uniform, however, means "like." This is one of the reasons that God created sergeants.

Sergeants do not get to make out assignments in most departments. Being in a supervisory capacity, they do little police work. This leaves a large, empty space in their day, which they fill up by nitpicking. You have a sergeant to make sure that you are in proper uniform. This means a tie, if ties are called for, and it means shiny shoes, just like everyone else. Patrolmen will tell you, "You can always tell a sergeant, but you cannot tell him much." Even if you do not see the stripes, you will know the sergeant. He will be the only officer wearing a hat at a crime scene and will be taking note of everyone who isn't. This is true in Knox County and in almost any department with more than two officers.

One other glaring problem with "Hill Street Blues" was that everyone kept ending up in bed with everyone else. This is not feasible among people who carry guns for a living. You do not fool around with another officer's wife, if for no other reason than survival. It should go without saying that you do not sleep with the captain's ex-wife, not if you ever want to pass another evaluation.

All in all, though, "Hill Street Blues" was among the more realistic shows. One show of bygone days had good technical direction, but lacked personality. "Adam 12" had the right radio lingo, and the writers were up on procedure. You never saw an officer lose his temper, though, and you never saw him drag a suspect behind a building to "question" him. You were left with the impression that cops are all clean-cut young men who would never utter a dirty word.

Real cops learn to speak the language of the gutters. The trend recently has been for police administrators to stress calm, courteous language. Cops are often disciplined when they step out of line. Modern cops are taught to avoid profanity because it lowers them in the eyes of offenders. I have to take issue with this.

A cop on the old "Sanford and Son" television series illustrates what I am about to say. He would ask a question something like, "Mister Sanford, was the perpetrator who absconded with your merchandise a Caucasian, or was he of the African persuasion?"

"Huh?" Sanford would respond.

The first officer's black partner would then translate, "He means, was the sucker who ripped you off a paddy or a brother?"

Cops deal with many people who think that *mother* is the first half of a word. A precise and correct officer will make a suspect more nervous than he already is. You have to "get down" with a suspect sometimes, then be ready to shift gears when you make your next stop, where the people may not be used to gutter talk. A cop must be able to communicate, no matter whom he encounters.

Most cops master the ability to shift from gutter talk to plain English. They learn not to say words like *fuck* in front of little old ladies. There are some, though, who eventually lose the ability to speak normally. Like old war dogs, they eventually have to be removed from the streets lest they totally wreck public relations for the department.

One such officer was a favorite of mine. Somewhere along the line he lost the ability to distinguish citizens from dirtbags. Let me explain further. As they advance through the years, most street cops categorize the world into three groups—other cops, citizens, and dirtbags. The last word varies from department to department and from year to year, but the attitude is the same. A citizen is subject to being reclassified when he begins to give a cop a hard time.

This officer (call him Mark) became so locked into gutter talk that even after he was repeatedly warned, he was unable to make the transition. He talked to teachers, principals, priests, and nuns the same way he talked to drug dealers and pimps. He became a legend one afternoon in court.

"Officer," the defense lawyer said with a knowing smile, "you say my client was driving in excess of the speed limit. *Exactly* how fast was that?"

"I didn't clock him on radar, but I know he was over thirty miles an hour, which was the speed limit," Mark replied.

"How fast would you estimate. . . ." the lawyer continued on, under the impression that he was dealing with an ordinary police officer.

"Look," Mark snapped, "I told you I don't know *how fast* he was goin', but the sonofabitch was haulin' ass!"

The courtroom erupted in laughter. The lawyer, red-faced, looked to the judge for help from an obvious barbarian. The judge, choking back a laugh himself, declared that an officer definitely should be able to tell if a suspect was "hauling ass."

His crowning achievement came one night as he was working an accident. On this particular night, Mark waved the same car through three different times. The fourth time he walked over to the rubbernecking driver.

"I'm trying to clear up this wreck," Mark said. "If you come through here again, I'll write you a ticket. Now get your ass away from here."

"I beg your pardon," was the indignant reply. "I happen to be a Knox County Commissioner. You will address me as such." A county commissioner is the same as a councilman or an alderman.

"Oh, *I am sorry* commissioner. What I meant was, get your *honorable* ass away from here before I write you a ticket."

Through the years, I have seen otherwise intelligent police officers do things that would rival anything a television writer could imagine. Cops entertain each other with such stories on slow night shifts.

The Reserve Unit of the Knox County Sheriff's Department consists of a fine group of men and women who take a lot of strain off regular patrol officers. Unfortunately, it is easier for a slightly unstable individual to slip into the reserve unit than to become a regular officer. They are not under day-to-day surveillance as are regular officers. One such reserve officer nearly caused heart failure among regular officers one early morning.

It was his first shift as a "senior patrolman." There was another reserve officer with him, but *he* was in charge. He received his first "hot call" early that Sunday morning. A bank alarm on a weekend would not have raised adrenalin in a regular officer because no one robs banks on weekends. It was his first call ever on which he was in total command, and he meant to do it well.

"I'm 10-97," he told the dispatcher in a professional voice, "everything appears Code J." It was the next sentence that woke up everyone from early morning drowsiness. "By the way," he said, almost casually, "start a another car over here. I passed an accident a quarter of a mile east of here. The car was in three pieces, and an individual with blood all over him tried to flag me down."

We all listened in horror, realizing that the night people all over the county were listening to their scanners, not to mention reporters. The first priority in any situation is an injured person. Fortunately, we found the injured man a little later. He had no life-threatening injuries, but he was still puzzled about why the first car had driven around him. The reserve officer left shortly afterward. I do not know if the hysterical laughter every time he came to roll call bothered him or not.

Even first-rate officers sometimes catch their tails in the door when they allow their better judgment to be affected by anger. I know from firsthand experience.

One rainy night I was called to meet another officer, to help him serve a warrant on the night shift. "Here's the situation," my fellow officer told me, "I've found this guy three times now. He runs like a deer. This time I intend to take him. About a mile down the road, you'll see three trailers, one in front of the other. He'll be in the first trailer. I'm going to pull around and block the back door. You drive through the front yard and up to the front door. I'll catch the bastard this time."

"It's pretty wet to be pulling into a yard," I told him. "Maybe we should go in on foot."

"Nope, he'll run if he sees us. Tonight he goes to jail. I've got good information. I'll take the responsibility for any damage. You just make sure he doesn't get out the front door."

A few minutes later I roared through the front yard, taking out a flowerbed not visible in the dark. I bailed out, covering the front of the trailer. A moment later I heard Carl pounding on the back door. "Come on out, John! This is the police! I know you're in there!"

"What's the problem, Officer?" A meek voice from inside asked.

"Send John Handel out. I know he's in there," Carl said.

"Officer," the quivering voice said, "John is staying in the trailer behind me, not here."

Before Carl could respond, a door slammed at the trailer behind him. A figure broke from the darkness and ran to the woods nearby. Carl was right. He *could* run like a deer. I looked at the damaged front yard and prayed fervently for mercy. The prayer apparently worked. The people did not complain.

Of all the cop shows ever shown on television, "T.J. Hooker," in my opinion, was the silliest. The most glaring inconsistency was the almost weekly pursuit in which Hooker always wrecks a police vehicle. During the pursuit, he will cause ten or fifteen accidents. You never see him doing any paperwork afterward.

In reality, Hooker would be placed behind a desk after the third or fourth demolished cruiser. No chief or sheriff could justify keeping an idiot like Hooker, who engages in high speed pursuits on crowded streets. The lawsuits alone would take up all the department's resources.

His automobile pursuits are only a little more ridiculous than his foot pursuits. We watch Hooker, who we know is old enough to have a grown daughter, chase youthful offenders for block after block. When he catches them, he still has enough wind left to subdue them or shoot it out.

A young, athletic cop might pull it off, but not a middle-aged man carrying twenty-five pounds of equipment.

Then there is the matter of the fist fights. The producers of "T.J. Hooker" are not alone in this error. It crops up in most cop shows and westerns. The simple fact is this: veteran officers do not punch hard surfaces—such as faces—with their fists. First of all, if you punch him out, you have to explain the damage done to your prisoner. Most important, though, *you cannot take chances on injuring your gun hand.*

This is not to say that no cop *ever* uses his fist as a weapon. Excitable rookies may do it without thinking. After a few broken knuckles and sprained wrists, though, it stops. Even with a legitimate solar plexus punch, there is a danger that your fist will encounter a large belt buckle or a weapon under a shirt. Try to punch it out with a well-trained cop, and you will find yourself on the receiving end of a nightstick.

Are cop shows realistic? Some are. Some are not.

Truth, they say, is stranger than fiction. Nowhere is this more obvious than when you start writing about cops.

25

When the Time Has Come to Buy the Farm

"**W**hat shift was working last night?" my wife asked.

"What?" I said sleepily, rolling over to look at the clock. Then I sat up in bed. I knew that 6:00 A.M. was too early for casual questions about shift assignments.

"What's wrong?" My heart was pounding.

"A county officer has been shot somewhere in the west end. They haven't released a name. What shift worked last night?"

"Charlie Shift," I said, pulling on my clothes. If the media had not released a name, there was a reason. They were making sure the family had been notified first. There would be no happy ending today. Four times since becoming a cop the news had reached me that an officer had been shot. The others had survived.

"Who runs west on Charlie Shift?"

"You don't know most of them," I lied. Steve Hensley. Carl Seider. Robert Lee. The names flashed through my mind. Whoever it was would be a friend. Some of them had sat at our table and had children who had played with our children.

"I'll let you know as soon as I find out," I told my wife as I went out the door. I knew the dispatcher would not

163

release the name, even to another cop.

Once in my cruiser, I went to the car-to-car channel. Generally it would have been filled with what administrators call "unneeded chatter." It was silent. The silence confirmed what I already knew.

It was a horrible way to wake up. Had I not been home, my wife would have been frantically calling around, trying to find out if I was on a slab at the morgue.

A few minutes later I spotted a cruiser backed into a hardware store that had not yet opened. He had a radar gun set up but was staring into space, ignoring the traffic. I saw the officer cringe as he recognized me. It was worse than I had thought. In a small department, officers know who is close to whom. The dead officer was a friend of mine, or at least someone the officer in the car thought was a friend.

"Who bought the farm?" I asked through a dry throat.

"It was Jim Kennedy," he told me with obvious reluctance.

Stunned, I sat staring. I had been prepared for the death of a Charlie Shift patrolman. The names were in my mind. I was steeled for the blow. But this was like being hit from the blind side. Jim was not on Charlie Shift. He was an investigator, recently promoted.

"How did it happen?"

"I don't know. Jim and another officer were trying to go through a motel door. They say Jim caught six rounds from a nine millimeter pistol."

That is still all I know. I could have asked any number of people, but I never did. It was irrelevant. Jim was twenty-nine, self-confident to the point of arrogance, had a wicked sense of humor, and was my friend.

A few weeks earlier we had pulled in behind an abandoned school building and talked over a pizza. We did not socialize off duty but spent a lot of time telling cop stories on slow nights. He was quick and intelligent. We kept a sniping contest going, each trying to have the last word about many subjects.

"They've posted an investigator's job," he said around a bit of pizza. "You gonna bid on it?"

"Naw, I'm not through being a street cop yet. You should, though, you've always been too dainty to wrestle with drunks anyway."

"You're fairly perceptive for an aging hillbilly," he answered. "At least you recognize my finer features."

"If I didn't, you'd certainly remind me. Modesty is not one of your faults," I told him, tearing off another triangle of pepperoni pizza.

"False modesty is not a virtue, Hunter."

"Then you must be full of virtue, or an arrogant pup like a lot of people say."

"Drop dead, Hunter. I'm going to put in my bid. What do I need, besides my more than ample qualifications?"

He put in his bid and got the job. Now, a few weeks later, it was open again.

At home that morning, I got out my scrapbook and turned to a picture of the previous Christmas. The picture was of David Shift and was shot for a Christmas promotion of the *Journal Milk Fund*. Jim was standing behind me, slightly turned to speak to someone. He was smiling his knowing smile. The heavy mustache, which he wore to make him look older, had never worked. He still looked like a very young man.

I saw confidence there, not only in Kennedy, but in all of us. We appeared ready to take on the criminal world alone, with twenty-five pounds of equipment and a six-shooter. Jim did not look at all like a ghost, nor did the rest of us. The picture brought mortality close to me that morning. One minute you are ready to fight the world. The next you are a memory in someone's scrapbook.

The general public tends to use euphemisms for the word *death*. Cop's are worse, though. Instead of *passed on* or *departed*, we say "He bought the farm," "They wasted him," "He cashed in his chips," "He bit the dust," or "He checked out." We must keep the real word at bay— D–E–A–T–H. Death is that shadowy figure who hitches a ride in your cruiser and sometimes becomes visible in the glow of your dashboard when you think too much.

Public mourning began the first day. All badges were covered with a piece of black ribbon. A small black flag flew from the antenna of every cruiser. It does not matter whether you knew the officer personally. One of your own has met a violent end. You do not want to be quickly forgotten, so you do not quickly forget. In a day or two, the press will have moved on to other stories, but the cops remember.

Jim Kennedy's death marked the end of one friendship and the beginning of another for me. I received a call from Mike Upchurch, fresh from the academy, still working in the jail. He was having car trouble and wanted a ride with me to the memorial service. We parked at the City–County Building and walked the few blocks to the church. There was a long line of blue, not only deputies, but city officers come to pay their respect, all walking silently, two by two.

My composure held until we arrived at the church, and I saw David Shift. The officers were standing in ranks by the door, wearing white gloves, at parade rest. The tears began to run down my face. It was *right*. The officers with whom you have served should see you off. They guarded your back, they came when you called for help. It was right and fitting that they should be there to say the last farewell.

A cop's funeral reminds everyone else of things they would rather forget—of young widows and small children without fathers and of vanished income. It reminds them of the pain their own families would be enduring. Most of all, I think, it reminds them that the shield they wear or carry in their pockets is only symbolic. It will not stop bullets.

As I took Upchurch home, we were silent for a long while. Almost at his house, he spoke. "Was Jim a good friend of yours?"

"Well, we didn't socialize, but he was my friend. He was a good cop. If he was covering your back, it was covered."

"I hear Baker Shift is short a man," he said.

"Yeah, we are. They should be posting it any time now."

"Would you talk to the captain for me? I'd like to work

on Baker Shift," he said.

"Why Baker Shift?" I asked.

"Well," he drawled, "I always say, if you're going to do a thing, do it right. Baker Shift makes almost as many arrests as the other shifts combined."

I watched him curiously out of the corner of my eye. We had just buried a cop, but even in the face of death Mike was anxious to be about his job. I did not really know him, though we had been in the reserves together.

"I don't have a lot of influence, but I'll talk to him. The captain wants hard workers. I guess the most important step toward being a 'Killer Bee' is to want it. Not everybody does." We had been nicknamed "Killer Bees" by Jim Brackett, our lieutenant, because of our high arrest rate and aggressiveness.

For whatever good it did, I talked to the captain. Shortly thereafter, Mike joined Baker Shift and we began a partnership and friendship that endures today. When Seth Rawlston and Mike Hailey transferred off, the captain put Upchurch on the wild and wooly Clinton Highway beat and made me the "Wild Car North," or backup unit.

So it goes. The job continues. If I buy the farm today, someone will step in and take my place. This is as it should be, as it must be. Still we must remember those who secured the ground with their blood.

The world will not remember that a cop died that night. It was not the Battle of Hastings or the invasion of Iwo Jima. It will not be a footnote in history books. It was not even a long newspaper story.

The Brotherhood will not forget you, though, Jim. We will remember for you.

26

They Joust With Windmills

Cops in general, and Southern cops in particular, have a touch of the romantic about them. They believe that the good guys always win, and they drive their cruisers the way knights once rode their horses. I have seen cops stand and cheer in a theater when the good guys win. Movies like *Walking Tall,* a movie about a Tennessee sheriff who took on corrupt forces, are favored viewing by officers.

Despite a touch of the romantic, most cops are hard-headed realists at bottom. Fuzzy thinking is not conducive to survival on the street; for the most part, the macho swagger is part of a show put on for civilians.

Cops are *supposed* to walk tall, tip their hats, and say "Mam" the way John Wayne did. They are supposed to exhibit a steely-eyed look to strangers. They do not let their public down.

Occasionally, however, the macho image gets out of hand. An officer becomes caught up in the fantasy, forgetting that cinematic cops are merely make believe creatures who will be resurrected at the end of the show. When this happens, the officer involved becomes a danger to himself and to others.

Generally, it is a temporary aberration, and the officer will snap out of it. There are individuals, however, who lose track of the light at the end of the tunnel. They begin to seek out and joust with windmills. Usually, a word from other officers puts them back on the track. Sometimes, though, they never get back to the center of the road. When that happens, it is only a matter of time until they are finished with police work.

In the following stories, identities have been carefully protected. They are true, but locations, descriptions, times, and even departments have been changed in order to assure that former officers are not recognizable.

"I want *you*," the State Trooper growled. "Outside."

The enormous man at the bar slowly turned, a look of disbelief on his face. At six feet, three inches, and well over two hundred pounds, he was still an impressive man, as he approached sixty years of age. Though pocked with ancient acne scars, his sun-burned face had a certain look of grandeur about it. He was an old warrior whose battlefield had been the bars and taverns of that highway for forty years.

Having been arrested numerous times, he held no animosity for the cops who had jailed him. It was part of the game. There were rules, however. Either the cops came in sufficient numbers to make it obvious that fighting was futile, or they discreetly asked him to step outside where the arrest could be made quietly. You certainly do not throw a challenge at a man in front of all of his friends unless you are prepared to go down to the wire. Any cop knows that.

"Are you talking to me, Pee Wee?"

The gauntlet had been hurled to the ground.

The trooper flushed. The old brawler's boots were older than the young cop. Walking through the bar, the trooper had overheard an unkind comment about his ancestry. Every cop hears those comments while walking through bars. You generally ignore them; to acknowledge that you heard is to bring on confrontation.

"Yeah, I'm talking to you, dirt bag. I want you outside, *now!*

170

Suddenly, everybody in the bar ceased talking. The young trooper had no idea what had gone wrong. All the old cops peppered their speeches with words like "dirt bag." What he did not understand is that it is a private word used among colleagues—not for people you intend to arrest.

"Piss off," the big man said, turning to pick up his beer.

The situation could still have been salvaged. The young trooper needed only to walk outside and call for help. Sheriff's Department cruisers were nearby. Upon the arrival of reinforcements, the man would have gone peacefully, his pride satisfied.

"You either walk out there," the trooper said in his best Clint Eastwood imitation, "or I'm gonna drag you out."

"Do it," the man said, sipping the can of beer.

"All right, I will!" The trooper stepped in, caught the man's arm, and attempted to take it behind his back in a "come-a-long" hold. It had always worked beautifully at the academy.

The arm did not budge. The man walked toward the door, the trooper straining at his arm. Someone opened the door, and the big man swung the hundred-and-sixty-pound officer outside. Every one of the bar patrons cheered.

The door flew open and the trooper re-entered, drawing his weapon. Again there was silence. "You're under arrest! Step outside!"

The big man turned his back on the young trooper. "Another beer," he said.

"I mean it! Outside, *now!*" The trooper was nearly frothing at the mouth.

"Boy, go ahead and shoot me, or put up that pea-shooter. Ain't nobody here impressed." It was not much of a gamble. Even enraged cops do not gun down people guilty only of misdemeanors. Finally the trooper retreated and called for help.

A few minutes later, Sheriff's deputies arrived to assist the indignant trooper. Inside, the big man turned to face them. He recognized the sergeant.

"Hello, Sarge."

"Hello, Asa. I guess you know why we're here."

"Yeah, but I ain't goin' nowhere with *him*."

"You got no choice, Asa. He says you were disorderly, drunk, and that you resisted arrest."

"He's a liar."

"You can tell the judge, Asa. Meanwhile, we're obligated to help him. Let's go."

"No," Asa said, stepping away from the bar as the deputies moved in on him. Moments later, he was dragged from the bar and put into the trooper's cruiser. Afterwards, the deputies stood straightening their uniforms. Asa had only put up a token battle—for the sake of dignity.

"Thanks," the trooper said.

"Officer," the sergeant said. "I have two suggestions for you. First, stay out of *this* bar from now on. You've lost face, and everyone you try to take out will fight back.

"Secondly, try to remember you ain't John Wayne. That uniform does not impress everyone. Don't try to do something you know you can't do. It'll get somebody hurt, and I don't want it to be one of my men!"

"Send a backup. I have four suspects in a vehicle with no tags on it!"

Monitoring the channel, I knew I was the officer's closest help. I turned on the siren and blue lights and screamed up the interstate in a pounding rainstorm. Four suspects, a lonely stretch of road, and no tag get the adrenalin flowing in a cop.

Matters were not helped when the officer failed to answer the dispatcher. I imagined him lying in a pool of blood in the pouring rain. Finally, I saw his blue-lights. Cutting across the median, I nearly mired up.

He was standing calmly in his rain gear, pump shotgun in hand, covering four men on the ground. The water washed over them in small rivers.

"What's wrong?" I asked.

"No tag. Foreigners. I think you may find weapons when you search the car."

Walking to the front of the vehicle, I found the temporary Texas tag right where it belonged. Walking back, I tried my best high school and army Spanish to inquire if any of them spoke English.

"We *all* speak English. We're American citizens," an indignant voice replied.

"Why didn't you tell the officer?"

"He didn't give us a chance. He just hollered on the loudspeaker and said he would shoot if we didn't do what he said."

"There's a tag on this car, and these people all speak English," I yelled through the wall of rain.

"Tell them," he said calmly, "to be more careful when they come through my county again." He put the shotgun in the front seat and drove away.

"You guys can get up," I said.

"What's *wrong* with him?" one of the dripping men asked.

"I have no idea. You can complain in the morning, if you want to."

"No thanks, *amigo.* I just want to get out of this county and never come back again!"

They were no more puzzled than I was. It occurred to me that the officer just might be seeing things that were not there. Eventually, everyone realized it. Fortunately, he left before his delusions caused any serious problems.

"Let me take the door," I whispered. Narcotics had called for a beat officer to assist in a raid.

"Go ahead," one of them said. We had managed to approach the house without being spotted.

The narcotics officers had a search warrant. Narcotics is perceived as "glamour" by the general public, and sometimes by patrol officers. Patrolmen mostly spend their days answering domestic disputes and writing reports. It was my first opportunity ever to make a dramatic entrance at the scene of a raid.

Drawing a deep breath, I drew my foot back and kicked just under the doorknob. There was no resistance whatsoever. My momentum carried me through the door, staggering into the middle of the living room, even before I could yell, "Police!"

Two men and a woman looked up, startled from the television program they were watching and shocked at the uniformed cop who had suddenly reeled into their house. The narcs ran in behind me and took custody of the suspects.

My face burning in embarrassment, I followed one of the narcotics officers through a doorway. We vaulted over a stairwell and dropped dramatically down to the next level, weapons in hand. A startled man in coveralls dropped his hammer as two pistols were shoved under his nose.

"I'm a carpenter," he choked out, "I . . . I don't even know these people."

Everything snapped into focus as we saw his sawhorses and power tools. He *was* a carpenter, hired to do renovations. The door lock from the front door was on a table.

I slunk away as soon as possible, wondering what the odds were that a cop would try kick open a door with no lock on it.

It was a few days before I got over the escapade. When there was another door to be kicked open, I left it to someone else. I was glad I did.

That door was reinforced with steel. It did not give even a fraction of an inch and left the unfortunate officer *vibrating* for several minutes, an expression of shock on his face.

I vowed, thereafter, to leave theatrics to theatrical people.

Hank (we'll use that name) would have written his own mother a citation. He would have patiently explained that if he gave her a break, his father would expect the same thing in a similar situation.

There was no middle ground for him, no gray areas. Everything was black and white. His dialog was straight out of the old "Adam 12" television series—precise, clipped, without embellishment.

While other officers lazily used such terms as *David, Edward,* and *George* to denote letters in their radio transmissions, Hank used the international codes: *Delta, Echo,* and *Geronimo.* When on a special assignment, even if it were only running radar, he would say that he was out on a special *mission*. He lived in the grip of television and movie cop techniques.

Hank hungered to be a sergeant, but never made it. He wanted to share his wisdom with other patrolmen. Whenever a new cop hit the streets near him, he shadowed the man until one of two things happened: the other officer did everything Hank's way or he asked for a transfer. There was only one way to do anything, and that was *his* way.

Eventually, though, a patrolman was assigned to Hank's end of the county who was not a rookie. The officer had been a military policeman and had worked for other departments. He did not need Hank's supervision. Hank, of course, had other ideas. He set out to make the other officer over in his own image.

The veteran ignored Hank for several months, until Hank brought the matter to a head one day. It started with an alarm at a credit union. It was what cops call a nuisance alarm; it went off frequently. To make matters worse, their were two credit unions in the same shopping center, and it was easy to be confused about which alarm was sounded.

Rolling in, the veteran officer quickly ascertained that it was a false alarm. He told the dispatcher to cancel Hank, who was en route. Hank, however, felt that *all* alarms had to be double checked. After all, someone might have a pistol to the responding officer's head.

As the other officer stood talking to a credit union employee inside the building, Hank appeared, weapon in hand. On tiptoes, he danced down the sidewalk—his back was to the other officer—peering in at the window of the *wrong* credit union. Passers-by watched curiously as the armed officer proceeded to crouch in front of the window on the crowded sidewalk.

Finally, the other officer tapped on the window behind Hank. Hank looked around, saw his fellow officer, then stood and holstered his weapon. Stiffly, he walked back to his cruiser.

A while later, Hank called the other officer for a meeting. Getting out of his cruiser, he pulled his chest up pompously and proceeded. "Officer, I know you don't like me, but if we are going to work together, we *must* learn to cooperate. As you know, I am an advocate of *invisible deployment*, and . . . ."

"Is that what you were doing at the credit union?" The other officer had finally lost his patience.

"That's correct," Hank said. "*That* was invisible deployment."

"Well, then, if there *had* been a real armed robbery in progress," he shouted, "*someone would have shot your invisible ass off!*" The officer squealed away, leaving Hank with his mouth open.

They slip through, these quixotic individuals, in spite of screening and psychological evaluations. Real cops know that there are dangers enough on the streets without manufacturing any more. You need not hunt for windmills when there are dragons waiting.

27

Chowhounds and Southern Cuisine

I was eighteen years old and freshly graduated from basic training when I first tasted pizza. That wonderful, spicy dish brought tears to my eyes. It was exquisite, especially to my southern-trained palate.

Pizza had been around Knoxville for several years. I had never eaten any because they served beer at the pizza establishments, and my father forbade me to enter any place that served beer. I never had enough nerve to defy him until I was eighteen and out of basic training. Even then, I did not let him find out that I had frequented a "dive."

In the mid-sixties the fast food franchises had not yet flooded Knoxville. You had the Orange Julius, serving hotdogs, McDonald's, Krystal, and two local chains similar to the Krystal. There was no Mexican, little Chinese, not even a roast beef establishment. You ate hamburgers, hotdogs, or "country."

Mind you, I am not knocking southern cuisine, except okra, maybe. I love southern-style country food. Only an infidel would turn up his nose at a meal of southern fried chicken, peas, mashed potatoes, gravy, and hot biscuits covered with real butter—an infidel or a health food nut. I am neither.

Knoxville is now an urbane and sophisticated city. My children do not believe there was ever a world devoid of taco stands, roast beef chains, and the like. They cannot imagine it any more than they can imagine a world without television. They look at me in disbelief when I tell them that I was nine years old before there was a television in the house.

My father was certain the Devil had invented television to keep people out of church on Sunday nights. Eventually, growing tired of finding his children at someone else's house, he bought an old round screen set. It received two of the three Knoxville stations, and someone had to hold the antenna in order to get a decent picture. My father saw "Gunsmoke" that first weekend, and after that we always had a television.

A cop evaluates his beat by the number of places where restaurants "take care" of them. "Take care" means anything from free, to half price, to extra large portions for regular price. It makes a lot of difference to an underpaid cop who may eat out ten or twelve times a week.

Not all cops are comfortable with this type of arrangement. I never have been, and any place that refused my money never saw me very often. Even when the owner's intentions are good, people resent courtesies to officers. Besides, it always smacked of extortion to me. Mine is a minority view. I am sure plump waitresses were flirting with the Praetorian Guards in Rome while giving them wine at half price.

One excellent restaurant on my beat constantly refused to let me pay for my food. It was an excellent place to eat, so I compromised. I left enough tip to cover the meal. It was a family place, so I figured the money ended up in the same place. One morning the owner came and sat at my table.

"Officer, I wanta know if I've made you angry, or has someone else done something to you?"

"How can you even ask that, Joe? I sometimes eat here twice a day."

"Yeah, I know, and I always say, 'no charge.' Then you

leave the money anyway. What's the problem?" I looked at the snowy-haired man and chose my words carefully.

"I feel uncomfortable with free meals. Some cops take advantage, and it makes me feel bad. That's the *only* reason I always leave the money."

"Who said anything about *free*? You ever heard of an armed robbery here? No. The criminals see cops in here, and they stay away."

"Joe, the county pays us to do that."

"Yeah, and did the county pay all the cops who stopped to talk with my father when he was dying? Young guys had better things to do than sit with an old man, but they was always here after work, telling him jokes and making him feel like somebody. How much extra did they pay you when you got yourself banged up over at the motel last week? You can't pay somebody to be a *good* cop. There ain't enough money in the world. When my father died, an officer came through that door and sat with me while I cried like a baby. He didn't have to do that.

"So what if a deadbeat takes advantage once in a while? I can afford it. It's my job to let you know that *somebody* appreciates what you guys do. So I'm telling you, if you can't accept my hospitality, find someplace else to eat."

That matter was settled then and there. It never came up again.

There is always, unfortunately, someone who *will* take advantage. One officer, who was an otherwise good cop, decided he had a right to eat at a discount. I learned this the hard way at a new fast food franchise one afternoon.

It was a cafeteria-style line. He was just ahead of me. The cashier rang up his order. An impressive man, he stood, eyebrows rolling together like thunderheads. "You don't give a discount to officers here?"

I would have crawled into a crack had I been able. The flustered cashier retreated, looking for her boss. In a moment, the manager came. He explained that he had merely forgotten to explain it to the clerk. "Tell your friends they're always welcome here. Please enjoy your meal on the house."

I thanked the manager, cheeks burning. It was not over, though. As we sat down, my fellow officer said, in a voice that could have been heard outside, "I don't believe these people. We risk our lives every day, and they can't spring for a buck and half discount."

The same officer invited me to a pizza place one night. I knew the policy there, so I went with him. "Let's see," he said, "bring two large pepperoni pizzas and a large order of lasagna. Also a pitcher of tea."

The waitress turned to leave. "Just a minute. Ain't you gonna eat, Hunter?" I ordered a small pepperoni pizza, but he ate half of it after inhaling his order. His appetite was a wonder to behold.

"You wanna go somewhere for dessert?" He asked.

The half-price discount abruptly ended at that place when an officer brought his entire family in, then argued with the manager about paying full price. The chowhounds always do you in.

One evening I was eating a delicious meal of eggs over easy, with sausage and toast. A woman I had never seen before approached the table.

"I'm the new manager," she said. "My brother is a cop over in Lexington. I want you to tell your friends, no charge for cops here."

"That's a nice thought," I told her, "but you'd better put a limit on it. Or at least, put the more expensive foods off limits."

"No, I won't do that. How much can one cop eat?"

She found out two days later when a couple of chowhounds descended on her. They ate twenty-eight dollars worth of steak and eggs for breakfast, then went back for lunch. Needless to say, the policy was quickly changed.

For the uninitiated, "chowhound" is an old military term. The chowhound centers his life around the mess hall. He is always the first in line. He eats anything and everything. He will generally sit and beg food from everyone else at the table. He is never filled up, no matter how much he eats.

I once shared a beat with a chowhound. Breakfast is the

high spot of the morning shift for a patrol officer. The hours between five and seven are generally quiet. If you have a pleasant person on the beat with you, it is an enjoyable time. A chowhound always ruins it, though.

Every morning shift I would drive around until I was certain he had already stopped for breakfast. I was constantly making excuses as to why I could not have breakfast with him. He would not have understood why I was embarrassed when he ordered "double everything," then haggled if anyone tried to charge him even the regular price.

One morning I waited until he was parked at a breakfast spot, then went up the road to a fried chicken franchise that served breakfast. It was not my first choice, but it was preferable to eating with a human garbage disposal unit. I was taking my first bite when I heard him ordering doubles. He arrived at my table carrying a plate heaped with scrambled eggs, home fries, and bacon. He sat down and began to shovel it in.

"Didn't I just see you eating breakfast down the road?"

"Yeah, but I probably won't go back again. The cheap bastard said he'd charge me full price if I ate more than four eggs. A man can't fill up on four eggs." *And a half gallon of coffee, plus four orders of bacon and six pieces of toast,* I thought.

Breakfast is the southern meal. It has been enriched the last few years with pastries, fruits, and home fries. Basically, though, it remains the same. Eggs over easy, hot biscuits, gravy, and ham, sausage, or bacon. To finish off, of course, there is jam, or honey, or molasses over a biscuit, with melted butter.

A few years ago my doctor ordered me to cease and desist from gumming up my arteries with such foods. I tried it for a while—until I caught my doctor at the Waffle House, eating a country breakfast that made my meal look insignificant.

I guess even doctors do not like to be thought of as infidels or Yankees.

28

The Torso Caper and Other Jokes

Most cops have a sense of humor bordering on the bizarre. I do not know if the type of person who gravitates towards police work is normally this way, or if the job does it to them. It is, however, almost universal among police officers. Some days when I relate a story of what happened on my shift to my wife, I'm surprised that she doesn't find it funny (even though I'm hysterical). It is even worse when you tell a funny story at a social gathering and find everyone (except other cops) staring at you with horrified expressions. At least your wife knows that *all* cops are warped, not just you.

Humor is an escape valve, and no person needs to laugh more than a cop. Find a humorless cop, and you have a person well on the way to a breakdown. The worse a situation, the more likely a cop is to joke about it. It is a self-defense mechanism that allows people in an insane profession to stay relatively sane.

One night at roll call the captain read a bulletin for a missing person. The man had left home with a *Colt* revolver in his pocket. After giving out the description, the captain read the note the man had left. It said, "Honey, this is good-bye. A man's gotta do what a man's gotta do."

The entire shift burst into hysterical laughter. One officer, wiping tears from his eyes, said, "He shouldn't have to shoot himself after *that*. He ought to die from *shame*."

The story did not strike my civilian friends as humorous. I can still drive officers anywhere in the country into gales of laughter with it. You just have to learn to see the humorous aspect of suicide notes.

A few years ago in a Tennessee city, a man decided to kill his wife. Fearing that he would not be able to make his escape before the police arrived, he wired himself with several sticks of dynamite. The wires from the battery were run to his left index finger and thumb. If touched together, they would ignite the dynamite.

Sure enough, the police arrived just after he shot his wife. He showed them the dynamite and explained what would happen if the two wires made contact. The officers began to back off. The man, however, apparently could not resist taking a shot at the officers with the semi-automatic pistol he had just used to murder his wife. Unfortunately, the pistol jammed as he fired at the officers.

You guessed it. He reached with his left hand to pull back the slide to clear the jam. When his finger and thumb contacted the metal pistol, boom! The man was scattered for blocks. This story causes officers to fall to the ground in hysterical laughter. If you do not find it humorous, then you can understand why there is a communication gap between cops and civilians in matters of humor.

As a rookie patrolman, I stopped for gas one morning at the service center. I went inside to tell cop stories and swap lies with my shift mates. The service center is a place to relax and unwind before going off shift. A few minutes later I went out to get my car. It was not there.

A cop knows his cruiser the way a mother seal knows her pup, even if there are thousands just like it on the beach. You do not have to read the "snitch number" on the side to spot *your* cruiser in a crowd of twenty cars. You know your cruiser by the length of the antenna and the tilt of the mirrors. The realization that my cruiser was not there hit me as soon as I walked outside. As I turned to make an inquiry, everyone hurriedly drove away.

Frantic, I ran to the back lot, hoping they had left it there. I knew it was a trick and that my cruiser was safe, but losing your cruiser is a little like losing one of your children in a crowded store. As I was searching, an obviously disguised voice came over the car-to-car channel on my portable radio.

"Try the Zayre's parking lot."

After a five-block walk carrying twenty-five pounds of equipment, I found my car. I knew that two people had to be involved, one to drive my car, another to take him back. I remained silent but watched for sly glances until I was certain I had both culprits pinpointed. They took their punishment gracefully when they were careless enough to let me get at both their vehicles one morning.

It is a frightening experience to turn your ignition switch and have all your lights and siren come on at one time. It is even worse when you reach for the switch and find that it is not on the equipment but is perched on the dash. No permanent damage, but it takes awhile to get the screaming siren turned off.

A certain ranking officer of the sheriff's department is known for his love of publicity. He was enraged to find a letter circulating through the department. The letter was addressed to him and alleged to be from the editorial staff of *Playgirl* magazine. It went something like this:

> Dear Lt. _____
>
> We have received your letter and picture. The staff has now stopped laughing long enough to reply. We regret to inform you that we will be unable to use your picture as one of our centerfolds, as we do not feel that there are too many seventy-year-old women among our readers.
>
> Sincerely,
>
> _____
> *Playgirl* Magazine

The officer was livid. He wanted to send the letter to the FBI lab for a fingerprint check. Finally, he swallowed hard and forgot about it. The culprit was never caught, though we all had a good idea who he was.

Another officer of my acquaintance read an article about a street cop who made a habit of eating driver's licenses as a prank on belligerent drivers. He was not actually willing to risk prosecution for destroying a license, but he came up with another plan. He found an old, expired driver's license and waited.

The night finally came when a belligerent and intoxicated driver pushed him too far. Reaching into the glove box, my friend took out a jar of peanut butter, liberally smeared the peanut butter on the license, then proceeded to eat it, licking his lips with gusto.

The episode was good for two laughs. He watched the belligerent drunk fall silent as the license was eaten. Then at the jail he got to watch the driver's face when the *real* license was produced from his property bag. "I swear, I saw him eat it," the bewildered drunk told the jailers. This, by the way, happened before Tennessee switched to plastic licenses.

A rookie at the Knoxville Police Department found himself with an unexpected passenger one night. The episode started when a citizen called to report a body in the road. The responding officers found a well-put-together dummy. It was so nice they hated to waste it. Loading the dummy in one of their cruisers, they lured the unsuspecting Bob Wooldridge—a transplanted Pennsylvanian—to a remote area. It was too good to pass up—a rookie and a gullible Yankee.

One of the officers engaged him in conversation while the other did the deed. Then they walked with him back to his cruiser, making sure he never got an opportunity to look in the back seat where the dummy was seated. They let him drive about two blocks before they called him.

"Car 52. Do you have a prisoner?"

"Negative," he replied.

"Then who *is* that in your cruiser?"

He looked in the rearview mirror, saw the dummy, and went berserk trying to get out of the car. Cops have a re-curring nightmare that they will one day end up with an armed suspect behind them. The two senior officers pulled up laughing so hard that tears were streaming down their faces.

"You bastards," the enraged rookie screamed. "You almost caused me to wreck my cruiser. You could have *killed* me!"

As he watched them laughing at his discomfort, a thought occurred to him. His face lit up.

"Has Charlie seen this dummy?"

"No," one of the laughing cops said, "you're the first."

"Let's call him over here," Wooldridge said, "and do it to him."

A few years ago we had a case in Knox County that was referred to as the "Torso Killing." Body parts were found in silver plastic garbage bags in various parts of the county. After the newspapers picked up the story, we found out just how common silver garbage bags are.

The department was deluged by calls from citizens who had found silver garbage bags alongside the road or in vacant fields. Every time we were sent to check a garbage bag, the press rushed to us. Finally the calls were not given over the radio. Officers were told to call in by phone.

All the bags were thoroughly checked. No officer, even the laziest, wanted to explain why he had missed body parts in a silver bag. We were relieved when it appeared that all the parts had been located, though calls continued to come in for days afterward. Late one evening the dispatcher had me phone in.

"Got another garbage bag for me to look through?" I asked.

"No, I've got an entire torso in a creek for you to look at," she said.

"All right, give me directions," I said. I was not impressed. Citizens see all kinds of things when the papers have been full of lurid details.

The location was way out in the boonies, so I had Mike Upchurch meet me at a point near our beat line. The sergeant, catching parts of our transmissions on car-to-car, called to see if we had a call or if we were goofing off. I assured him that we had a call but would not transmit it over the air. He said he would head that way and call us when he was near.

"Right down there in the curve," the elderly woman said, "off the road in that swampy field. The kids seen it first, then called me. It's a dead woman with no head or arms."

Upchurch and I glanced at each other. It was obvious that the woman *believed* she had seen a body. People followed at a distance as we drove down to the curve. We got out and looked across the swampy field.

"I'll be," Upchurch drawled, "it *does* appear to be a torso."

"Have you arrived yet?" Our sergeant rasped over the car-to-car channel.

"Ten-four," I answered. "It appears that we have a torso in the creek."

"Don't touch *anything* until I get there," he said, "not anything."

"I always trample over murder scenes," Upchurch said. "Don't you? I would never have remembered to preserve the evidence if the sergeant hadn't reminded me."

"Don't be so hard," I laughed. "If sergeants couldn't give advice once in a while, they wouldn't have anything to do."

"Must've been in the water for a while," Upchurch said. "She's turning black."

"I'll bet she's real stiff by now," Mike said, staring intently from about twenty feet away. To my horror, he bent over and picked up a rock, then threw it at the torso. It bounced off with a *thud*.

"It's a department store mannequin," Upchurch chuckled.

We jumped down into the creek and picked it up. Carrying it between us by the hollow neck and leg section, we walked back toward the road. As we approached the pavement, the sergeant pulled up. A thousand different expressions crossed his face as he saw the mannequin we were carrying.

"I *told* you. . . ." he began. His mouth opened as we tossed the mannequin on the pavement. It skittered loudly toward him.

"Rigor mortis has already set in," I told him.

"Get back in service," the sergeant said, recovering as best he could. Sergeants do not like to appear less than perfect. He quickly drove away.

"I never would have gone back to work," Upchurch said. "I probably would have stayed down here the rest of the shift if it hadn't been for the sergeant."

I loaded the mannequin in my trunk. At the first opportunity, we put it in Denny Scalf's cruiser with a note suggesting deviant sexual practices. Eventually, I gave her to a Knoxville city policeman, who screamed into a hospital emergency room one night with the mannequin under a sheet. Then I lost track of her. I do have a picture, though, of Denny standing next to her. It is labeled the *Torso Caper*. Denny has his arm around her and is smiling.

Another example of twisted humor? Maybe. Never begrudge a cop any kind of humor, though. He needs all of it he can get.

29

Br'er Fox and Other Critters

"**N**orthend units," the radio crackled, "intruder at Commerce Bank, Highway 33. The complainant says someone is in the bank with her."

"Baker 10," I inquired, "can you advise on weapons or other details?"

"Negative. The complainant seemed to be hysterical. She told us that someone was in the bank with her, then hung up."

The call made no sense at all. There are no bank robberies at night. State-of-the-art alarm systems and near impregnable bank vaults have made burglaries a thing of the past. Besides, would a bank robber allow the complainant to use the telephone?

I rolled in and stopped a safe distance from the bank. My supervisor pulled in on the other side. There did not appear to be any action inside. Getting out of my cruiser, I racked a round into my shotgun. The supervisor and I walked cautiously up to the door.

Without warning, the front door flew open and a woman ran out shouting, "Get him! Get him! He's under the desk!"

The woman ran by without stopping. I looked at the

supervisor. Under the desk? The call was becoming more bizarre by the moment. We entered, sweeping the room with our eyes, then began to search methodically. We found the intruder under the third desk.

He was grayish-brown, about eight inches long, had no arms or legs, and hissed defiantly as we carried him outside. It was a garter snake that had somehow made it across one hundred yards of pavement from a nearby wooded area, searching for whatever it is that garter snakes search for.

A police officer who works rural beats is never very far from a wooded area or a creek bed. In the extreme north end of Knox County where I spent most of my patrol career, I was near the boundaries of a large state park. I had more "critter calls" than most.

On a particularly slow night shift, I ranged toward the outer limits of my beat, areas where we seldom went because we received few calls. As I dropped over a hill, a rabbit ran under my wheels. The whistling scream was nerve-wracking, and I turned to go back, fearing that I had left it crippled and in agony.

As I topped the ridge, I found out why the rabbit was running. A red fox stood over the cottontail. He was staring directly into my headlights, momentarily stunned by the unexpected brightness.

I had seen foxes in the zoo, but it was not the same. The moment was magic. The wily creature of the night stood staring, his black nose delicately sniffing the air. There was no panic in the glittering black eyes, only alert curiosity. Suddenly I knew why these creatures had survived so well, even in populated areas. The wisdom of the ages was in its eyes.

Then, with an almost delicate movement, the fox picked up the rabbit and vanished into the underbrush beside the road. Its movement was more feline than doglike. I sat for a moment holding my breath.

Though rarely seen, the fox is known to inhabit East Tennessee in great abundance. A cousin of the fox, however, caused me some serious kidding for several months, until

I was rescued by the Fish and Game Commission and an article in the Knoxville *News-Sentinel*.

An alarm came in about 3:00 A.M. at a clothing factory in the little community of Powell, Tennessee. The entire business was surrounded by a ten-foot chain link fence. I rolled up and hit the lot with my spotlight. A medium-sized animal, which I took to be a dog, was trotting around the inside the fence.

"Baker 10," I said, "have the security company get a guard out here to open the gate. Also, tell them one of their dogs has gotten out of the building."

I drove around the outside of the fence while I waited for the guard to show up, but I could see no breaks. The animal continued to trot briskly around the inside perimeter of the fence, without pause.

"Baker 10, the guard is en route, but the security company advises that they have no dogs at that location. They further advise that the alarm is coming from the lot, not the interior of the building."

I turned on my takedown lights for a better look at the animal. By this time it was panting, its long tongue hanging out. As I watched, it suddenly dawned on me: the animal was a coyote. Wolves and coyotes never look like the pictures you see of them. They look like dogs. This one was buff-colored, with darker hair running down its back. As I approached for a closer look, I saw that it was a female with swollen teats.

Driving around to the back of the building again, I found the coyote's point of entry. Dusty pawprints on the hood of a truck told the story. She had jumped up onto the truck, then jumped the fence to get at some tasty morsel in the dumpster on the other side. The leap back was too much for her.

"Sonofabitch," the security guard said as he got out of his car, "that looks like a wolf."

"Coyote," I said as we opened the big metal gate.

"Must be somebody's pet. We don't have coyotes here." The animal trotted past us without even looking in our direction, as though by ignoring us we would cease to be there.

"No, that's a wild animal. Look, she doesn't even know what a gate is."

"You gonna have her picked up?" he asked.

"Naw, I don't believe in locking up the innocent. When she gets back around here, let's herd her through the gate."

As she approached us, we jumped in front of her, yelling and waving our arms. She veered away through the gate. A moment later, realizing she was outside the fence, she loped away into the night to tell her cubs, no doubt, *never* to jump chain link fences.

The other officers on my shift laughed at me mercilessly when I told them about the coyote. They howled and snickered. Everyone knows we do not have coyotes in East Tennessee. We would have seen them. Had I seen any dragons or unicorns?

Finally, I called the fish and game people and talked to a ranger. He was not in the least impressed. "Yours is the first eyewitness account in that particular area," he told me, "but I'm not surprised. They've been moving east for years now. We estimate about 15,000 statewide."

"How can they live this close without anyone seeing them? This one had a litter somewhere."

"It takes a crafty animal to increase its population and expand its territory while other species are dying out. We won't see too many of them, even when they have a fairly high population density. They're just too smart."

When the *News-Sentinel* ran an article on the coyote population in Tennessee, I clipped it and made sure everyone saw it. When I later told them about the large owl I had encountered walking down a back road, only one person asked if he was in the company of a "pussycat." By the time I found the raccoon setting off a warehouse alarm almost nightly, there were hardly any giggles at all.

Seafarers will tell you that you seldom see any unusual creatures as you ply the oceans in large, noisy ships. Go out on a raft, though, and blend with your surroundings, and things begin to appear. It is the same with wild creatures of the forest. You must go where they live and be out when they are prowling.

Foxes, coyotes, raccoons, ponderous opossums, even bobcats: I have seen them all at one time or another in the backyards of people who have no idea they are there. All this is available to the southern officer, if he will take the time to get away from the neon lights and be quiet for a few minutes.

Wild animals are not the only creatures encountered by rural southern cops. "Baker 10, cows in the road." This is not an uncommon call. Mind you, there is no departmental policy dealing with cows in the road, but we always get them moved. It is easier than working accidents. Vehicles that collide with an animal the size of a horse or cow do not fare very well.

Marvin Reed, a Knox County officer, once herded a pack of llamas down a back country road after they escaped from an experimental farm. Knoxville city police once were called on to herd an angry ostrich back home. On rare occasions, a black bear will wander in from nearby Sevier County where the Smoky Mountains are located and wreak havoc with garbage cans and dogs, until captured and returned home. A southern cop never knows what animal is coming next.

The "cows in the road" call I received early one morning turned out to be a vast understatement. There was a whole herd of cattle, on several roads. My beat partner, Mike Upchurch, came over to help. After an hour or so, we had most of them driven back inside fences. I was congratulating myself on our success when I topped a ridge and met the bull.

He was big and red. That was the first impression. Next I noticed the large spread of horns that he showed me while snorting and pawing the ground. I had the distinct impression that he was not impressed by my badge, that he did not appreciate having me annoy his harem, and that he had no intention of going back inside the fence.

There was no place to run. My nightstick would be about as effective as a toothpick. The .38 revolver I was wearing could eventually kill the bull. However, I knew

195

from having dispatched injured animals before that I would have long been trampled to jelly before the bullets did more than just annoy him.

The tension grew. The bull seemed to be savoring the moment. Without really thinking, I threw up my arms and charged at him, screaming obscenities at the top of my lungs. My father always said, "Do *something*, boy, even if it's wrong."

The startled bull understood my tone, if not the content of my words. He whirled around and jumped the remaining strand of barbed wire where the cows had escaped. When Upchurch arrived, I was wiring the fence back together.

"What was the yellin' about?" he drawled with a voice like cold syrup.

"*That*," I said, "was a classic example of the command voice, delivered in the bovine tongue." Upchurch did not ask what I meant. He never does when I talk nonsense.

One incident that stands out in my mind, concerned an injured horse. We found him standing in the middle of a four-lane road on three legs, the other having been torn off by a vehicle. He was screaming in agony. There are few sounds more horrible. I quickly shot him to end the torment.

Later, as I filled out the shooting report, I could not resist injecting a little humor, despite still being sick at my stomach from having shot the horse. The shooting report assumed a human target, making no allowances for other types of shootings. Rather than simply dating it and attaching an incident report, I filled in the blanks as written. VICTIM'S NAME: Dobbin Horse, alias. FATAL OR NON-FATAL: Fatal. NUMBER OF SHOTS FIRED: Three. LOCATION OF WOUNDS: Behind the right ear, point blank. REASON FOR SHOOTING: Subject was obstructing traffic.

"Very funny," my supervisor said, handing the report back to me. "It's guaranteed to give someone in the front office a heart attack. Now, write an incident report and attach it to a shooting form."

Only in the South! And only a country cop has the opportunity to take part in animal husbandry. The night my hand was trampled by a horse, I did not file a report. I soaked my hand in hot water and hoped it would get better. It was easier than explaining *why* a horse had stepped on my hand.

30

A Pit Bull Named Rocky and Other Dogs

The call had come in as a domestic dispute in progress. I wound my way through the wooded area, looking for a house that fit the proper description. Deputy sheriffs working rural beats seldom have proper house numbers to go by. I was also completely out of radio contact in the valley where I was driving.

Then I saw it. The house was what is sometimes called a "shanty." The outside walls were covered with tar paper, and there was no foundation as such. It sat on stacks of concrete blocks.

Pulling in the driveway, I watched for movement. You never know what to expect in a domestic dispute. Stepping from the cruiser and starting for the porch, I suddenly found myself facing a white pit bull that weighed about eighty pounds. Being very familiar with the breed, I stopped dead in my tracks.

A dog that barks is nervous. This dog sat staring at me, without moving. He obviously was not insecure about his ability to contend with a mere police officer with a gun and a long stick. A dog that behaves in this manner is not a dog to be trifled with.

I stood still for perhaps a minute. For all I knew, an enraged, drunken husband might come charging from the door with a shotgun poised for action. On the other hand, I was certain the dog would attack if I attempted to cross his domain. The only sure way to get a pit bull loose once he gets a good hold is to put the gun in his mouth and fire—assuming, of course, you do not pass out from the pain before you get your gun out.

The door opened and a woman with stringy hair came out, pulling on a worn housecoat. "He's gone," she said. "He'll be calmed down when he comes back."

"Would you do something for me, please. Call the Sheriff's Department and tell them that Baker 10 is all right. And would you take your dog inside?"

"Come here, Tonto," she said. The dog got up lazily, looking at me as if to say, "You lucked out this time, Jack."

The woman returned a few minutes later, leaving the dog inside. "I called in for you," she said.

"Thanks. Now are you going to be all right, or. . . ." A small bundle of fawn-colored fur charged from under the porch and grabbed me by the cuff of my trousers. It was a pup, about eight weeks old. He worried the cloth of my pants as if he intended to drag me down.

I picked him up. He growled ferociously as I looked him in the face. "Is this pup related to the dog inside?"

"The one inside is his father. Mother's a mongrel, though, half pit and half German shepherd."

"Would you sell me this pup?" I asked on impulse. He reached out and licked my face, as if understanding what had happened. I knew then that his name was Rocky.

"You can have him," she shrugged. "We got no use for a mongrel. You can't fight 'em . . . . I mean, you can only enter purebred dogs in a show."

Things fell into perspective. There were no show dogs being bred here. The woman's husband apparently fought his dogs. Though felonious in most states, dog fighting thrives in many.

"Thanks," I said, "if it's all right, I'll pick him up Saturday morning. By the way, if you need us again, just call."

Most police encounters with dogs do not end with the dog going home with the policeman.

The dog is a territorial animal who does not differentiate between police and other humans. I found this out one morning while participating in a fugitive hunt on foot. Walking into a clearing, I came face to face with a hundred-pound German shepherd. The dog bristled and growled.

"Good dog," I said. He growled louder. I stood stock still until the Knoxville Police Department officer emerged from the woods.

"I thought you were the fugitive," he said, snapping the leash back on. The dog immediately relaxed.

"Isn't he trained to recognize a uniform?" I asked.

"Nope. The criminal might have on a uniform tomorrow."

I never forgot that bit of information. A Chattanooga rookie, however, found out the hard way that police and guard dogs cannot tell the good guys from the bad guys.

He was responding to an alarm at a lumberyard. Rookies tend to be enthusiastic to a fault. He jumped from his cruiser, just ahead of everyone else and sprinted for the fence. With his brother officers, who had been there before, yelling for him to wait, he jumped in the back of a pickup truck parked by the ten-foot chainlink fence, jumped to the cab, then vaulted over the top of the fence onto a stack of lumber.

The other officers looked at each other as he disappeared in the dark, heading for the office area. Moments later, he reappeared, with two Dobermans in hot pursuit. He made it to the top of the lumber pile, but as he was going for the fence, one of the snarling Dobermans took out the seat of his pants.

"Charlie," one of his giggling cohorts said as he stood ashen and gasping for breath, "what we wanted to tell you is that there are guard dogs inside the fence. They probably set the alarm off."

Another officer was not so lucky in this story related to me by a dog trainer. He was part of a team sent to a house to make an arrest. He was on the front porch when a snarling German shepherd hurtled across the yard and hit the porch with screeching toenails.

Forgetting why he was there for the moment, the officer climbed one of the porch columns, drawing his legs up as far as he could. The shepherd began to leap in the air, grabbing at his feet.

Slipping downward into the jaws of the dog, the officer drew his weapon in desperation, aimed downward and shot himself twice in the leg. The shepherd, unhurt, but frightened by the noise, fled the scene.

I would love to have read that report.

Generally, I have gotten along with dogs pretty well. It's simply a matter of learning how to behave around them. I do not smile at a strange dog. To a dog, bared teeth means a snarl. I also try not to run, but learn to be calm.

None of this matters, though, if a dog has been trained to disregard its instincts. I found this out one night when Mike Upchurch and I were dispatched on a car burglary in progress.

This particular thief had made two mistakes that night. He was drinking on the job, which meant that he was not as alert as he should have been. The second mistake was to steal in his own neighborhood. He knew better, but the shiny new car had been too much temptation. It had a valuable tape deck worth a considerable amount of money.

People inside the house saw him and called the Sheriff's Department. He was still inside the car when Upchurch and I slid into the yard. Moments later we were in foot pursuit.

Showing great brilliance, he ran directly to his house, with the two of us less than twenty feet behind. He ran through the front door and attempted to slam it on us. Upchurch kicked it open, and we followed him in.

As we went through the door a dog—without bark or growl—leapt across the room at us, coming in at face level. It looked like a cross between a German shepherd and an Airedale terrier. At the moment, though, all we could see were teeth.

On reflex, I swung my flashlight. It was a police light

202

made of heavy cast aluminum and containing six "D" sized batteries. The tip of the light hit the dog right between the eyes. He hit the floor, staggered for a moment, and then fled to the kitchen, falling down several times.

Moments later, Upchurch had cuffed the suspect and read him his Miranda warning. As we were about to leave, Upchurch saw the dog. It was peeking from behind the refrigerator at us.

"Is your dog bad to bite?" Upchurch drawled.

"He *used to be*," the thief said in disgust.

It was the worst snowstorm we had experienced in years. The heavy winds may have explained why the two burglars inside the bar had not heard Chester Slagle's cruiser as he pulled in behind their van and saw that the bottom of a door had been kicked in. Moving in closer, he could hear the burglars as they leisurely pilfered the bar, probably figuring that all wise policemen would be inside out of the weather.

Skeeter, as Chester has been called from time immemorial, called for backup. A monster-sized man, he nonetheless followed procedure.

In a few minutes Steve Hensley and I, who had been chatting behind a shopping center a few miles away, and David Lively arrived. Moments later, we were in place. The noise had stopped by that time. The burglars had heard us.

"Come out with your hands in front of you," Skeeter yelled. "Police officers."

There was silence. No one came out. We all glanced at each other. In the police movies, cops always kick in the door heroically. Real cops know better. With sudden inspiration, Steve Hensley barked like a dog.

Glancing up, Skeeter caught on immediately. With a grin, he yelled, "Come out, or we're sendin' in the dogs!"

I immediately joined in with my own snarling and growling. "Down boy!" Skeeter yelled. "Hold on to them!"

"We'll come out!" A near hysterical voice yelled from inside. "Hold the dogs! Don't shoot."

We scooped up the first thief as he came out on his hands and knees and cuffed him. The second man soon followed.

A short time later, they were sitting in the car having their rights read to them. As Skeeter was about to shut the door, we all heard a scuffing noise on the icy parking lot. A skinny old hound that had meandered around the building stopped to stretch and yawn, then looked curiously at all the people standing amidst the flashing blue lights, as if wanting to know why we had disturbed his sleep.

"*See?*" One of the thieves said. "I told you it was a *real* dog."

After the near hysterical laughter ended, we took the thieves to jail.

31

'Tis the Season to Be Jolly

"**W**e've almost made it," I said, "Ten more minutes and the shift is over."

"Yep," Mike Upchurch said, "we've just about made it through."

"Just remember," Jim Brackett, our lieutenant, said, "it ain't over until it's over. Ten minutes can be a lifetime in this business."

It was Christmas Eve of 1984. We had started the shift at two in the afternoon determined to have a pleasant Christmas. Filled with the Christmas spirit and anxious to go home, we had spent the day *warning* violators, then sending them on their way with a "Merry Christmas." Nobody likes to make an arrest on Christmas Eve.

"Baker 16," the dispatcher said, "fight in progress." She gave an address a short distance from where we were sitting.

"A fight," Upchurch growled. "I can't believe it."

"I can't believe the location. That's the black family at the end of the road. Those are the most law-abiding people on the beat," I added.

"Happens in the best of families," Brackett said. "Too much to drink and old problems pop up. Let's do it." We got in our cruisers and were on the scene in less than a minute.

An elderly woman met us at the door. "Hurry," she said. The neat little frame house was a wreck. Furniture was overturned, and lamps lay in the floor. From down the hallway we could hear the sounds of struggling.

In the back bedroom one female sat astride another, pounding the second woman's head on the floor. Had it not been carpeted, the woman's head would have been mush. A man of thirty or so stood behind them, blood running from a cut on his forehead. The lieutenant picked up the first woman and carried her out of the room by the waist. She was sobbing with rage.

"Do ya'll have some kind of problem here?" Upchurch drawled. It was obvious that he had an irrational hope that someone would say "No" so we could leave.

"*Do we have a problem?*" The man asked, wiping blood from his face. "My sister done wrecked Momma's house, hit me in the head with a bottle, and tried to kill my wife!"

"Other than *that*," Upchurch said, "do you have a problem?"

"Ain't that enough? Put that woman in jail. She do this every year. She hate my wife, and every time we comes from Michigan for Christmas, my sister starts this up."

"You don't really want your sister in jail for Christmas," I said. "After everyone calms down, you'll regret it."

"I want her out of here, now," the man said. "She can't git along with nobody."

"What if we work something out," I said. "Let someone take your sister home. Then the rest of you can still enjoy what's left of the evening."

"How am I supposed to have a good evenin'?" the woman on the floor said, sitting up. "She done give me a headache and pulled out half my hair. Put her in jail!"

"All right," I played my ace in the hole, "but you have to go downtown and sign the warrant."

"Why should I be put out? She done caused the problem. She jealous of me."

"You're the victim," I said. "That's the way it works." I

206

did not mention that we had grounds for a disturbing the peace charge.

In the living room the sister-in-law was sobbing, but she had stopped struggling with the lieutenant. "It be the same every year. She come in braggin' about her fancy house and clothes. This year she braggin' about the new Buick they drivin'. She nothin' but a uppity bitch."

"You just jealous," the offended woman yelled from the bedroom, "because you married to a triflin' man that can't git a better job than shovelin' asphalt."

"That's enough," Upchurch said, "Don't start it back up again."

"Can anybody take this woman home?" the lieutenant asked.

"I'll take'er home, officer. She's my wife," said a man who had been watching and listening quietly. "She git a little upset when she been drinkin' wine."

"If you was any kind of man, you wouldn't let her talk to me like that. She right. You is triflin'," the sister-in-law said.

"That's enough," Brackett said. "Either leave with your husband, or go to jail. We're not here to referee a fight."

The woman's husband got her coat and gathered up Christmas presents. We checked the bleeding man and found that it was a very small cut. Walking behind the still sobbing sister-in-law and her husband, we herded them out the front door.

On the front porch, something set her off again, probably the new Buick parked in the driveway. She picked up a crockery flowerpot and hurled it toward the door, barely missing my head.

"That's it," Upchurch said, taking the cuffs from his belt. "You're under arrest for disorderly conduct and assault on an officer." The last charge was for emphasis. He knew I was not about to drive to jail on Christmas Eve. While the rest of the shift was opening presents, Upchurch was booking the angry woman.

That Christmas Eve was still an improvement over my previous one. I was a DUI Enforcement Officer, working 10:00 P.M. to 6:00 A.M. every night except Sunday and Monday. It was about 3:00 A.M. on Christmas Eve when I turned up a side road on my way to the highway for a cup of coffee.

As I climbed the curving road, I heard a four barrel carburetor kick in down the road behind me. The engine was screaming as the driver shifted gears. I could tell by the sound that the vehicle was traveling too fast to be under control, so I pulled onto the shoulder and stopped.

Moments later an old Chevrolet rounded the curve on screaming tires. Seeing my cruiser, he hesitated momentarily, then turned off his lights and screamed away. I had no intention of pursuing any vehicle on Christmas Eve, especially not a person who was evidently drunk or insane. I radioed other units to be on the alert and pulled back on the road. Moments later, I heard the horrible sound of a crunching impact.

As I rounded another sharp curve, I saw the car buried in an embankment. The rear end was just settling down, the air filled with dust. The nineteen-year-old driver was fifty feet in front of the car. He had crashed through the windshield, narrowly missing a telephone pole in his path. The passenger was lying half-in and half-out of his door. He had been swung backward by centrifugal force as the rear end swung around.

Flooding the area with light, I called for ambulances and assistance. The boy by the car had grey matter showing on his forehead. He was barely breathing. I could hear the driver drawing long, gasping breaths as I approached. White bones were visible where the collarbone had come through the flesh.

"Oh my God," I heard a male voice say. One of the neighbors had run outside in his pajamas. "Were you chasing them?" he asked. There was accusation in his voice, as if I were responsible for the stupidity of the driver.

"No, but I *should* have been," I said angrily. "He was endangering innocent people."

"Sorry, I didn't mean to sound critical. I know these things happen. It just seems a shame on Christmas Eve."

"It's a shame anytime," I snapped, checking the driver's

airway for obstructions, "but it happens frequently." It was obvious that the man still thought I had been chasing the car.

An hour later the vehicle had been removed and the ambulances were gone. The investigating officer took my statement. "The driver's nineteen, and the passenger's seventeen. They sure screwed up Christmas for their parents, didn't they?"

"They haven't done much for mine either," I said.

"It wasn't your fault. If you'd been chasing him, it still wouldn't have been your fault. The driver did it. If he had met a car, he could have killed a lot of people."

I got some coffee and hid behind a shopping center for the rest of the shift, fearing a repeat of the incident. Other people were at home, sleeping; I was scraping kids off the street. It did not make me feel any better to know that the other officer was right. I was a victim, too.

Both boys lived. Upchurch has arrested the driver for drunk driving since then, and the passenger has been involved in at least two accidents. The brain damage he suffered is controlled with medication.

Christmas is the season to be jolly, unless you happen to be a cop or are lonely. In 1985 I pulled up behind a huddled individual on Interstate I-75. It was a cold Christmas Eve, and I motioned for him to get in the back.

"It's not against the law to walk on the interstate, is it?" He was defensive.

"Matter of fact, it is. But all I was going to do was offer you a ride up to the truck stop."

"You ain't gonna arrest me, are you? Normally I wouldn't care, but tonight I'm going to Lexington to be with my daughter and her family." He was short, with the leathery look of a man who has been in the open a long time. His clothes were mission issue, clean but ill-fitting.

"I'm not going to put you in jail." I opened the door, and he got in.

"Sure is cold," he said.

"Yeah, and it'll be colder in the mountains. You should be able to find a trucker going north, though. I was about to have supper. Why don't you join me?"

"Officer, I know you mean well, but I just don't feel like charity tonight. I'll even admit that I'm a little hungry, but I started off new this morning and I ain't gonna start begging the first day."

"Say, do I look like a soft touch? I just hate to eat by myself. They give me half price at the truck stop, anyway."

"All right, I'll let you pay for my meal, but I'll mail the money to you when I find work. Damn if I don't feel like I could whip the world tonight."

"When was the last time you saw your daughter?"

"It's been six years. It was the night she got married. I got drunk and made a jackass of myself. Up to then, I was still working. After that, I drifted away and was ashamed to go back."

Inside, we ordered open-faced roast beef sandwiches with mashed potatoes and gravy. When he was almost finished, I ordered pecan pie. It was obvious he had not eaten for awhile. He washed the meal down with four cups of coffee.

"I want your name and address," he said. "I'm gonna send your money to you, and I'm gonna write your boss and tell him what kinda cops he's got out here."

"Just pass it on to someone else who needs it," I said, handing him one of my business cards.

"You've done a lot for me, officer. There's something else I need, but I hate to ask." He dropped his eyes to the table.

"So ask," I said.

"My daughter don't know I'm coming. She might not even talk to me. Would you call her?" He handed me a tattered scrap of paper with an address and phone number on it.

"I'll lend you the money, but I think you should make your own call."

"I can't do it," he said, "but I *have* to know."

"All right, I'll do it." I got up and went to the phone at the back of the truck stop. Fishing out the coins from my pocket, I made the call.

"Hello," the woman at the other end said.

"This is Officer Hunter of the Knox County Sheriff's Department. Is this Linda?"

"Yes. Are you calling about my father?"

"Yes, I am."

"Is he dead?"

"No, he isn't. He's here with me at a truck stop in Knoxville. He wants to come home for Christmas."

"Tell him to stay away from me."

"Ma'am. . . ."

"Don't you *dare* sound disapproving," she began to sob. "You don't know what it was like all these years, wondering if he was alive. Not a single word, not even a postcard. I won't let him do the same thing to my children. Tell him to stay away!" The phone went dead.

He approached. "Well, what did she say?" I have never seen such hope in a human face.

"She said the light will be on," I told him. As I watched his face begin to glow, I hoped God would consider my motive when I had to answer for that lie. It was possible his daughter would change her mind after she had time to consider it. I could not deprive a man of his only hope on Christmas Eve.

"Thanks," he said, wringing my hand, "there'll be some changes in this old drunk now." A little while later, I watched him climb into a northbound truck.

I was still thinking about the old man when I went back to work the day after Christmas. There was a note in my box to contact an officer with the Kentucky State Police. I explained who I was, and the investigating officer was on the phone in a few minutes.

"I appreciate your returning my call," he said. "I have a dead man here. We found him Christmas morning in a field just off I-75. Coroner says natural causes, but we can't identify him. The only thing he had in his pockets was one of your business cards. I was wondering what you could tell me about him?"

"I bought him a meal Christmas Eve. Just a minute. I have his daughter's name and number." I had forgotten to give it back to him.

"That's great," he said, taking the information. "Now I can finish my report."

"Trooper, which way was he traveling?" I asked.

"North, it appears. He was on the northbound side, anyway, south side of Lexington."

"Thanks a lot," I said.

Relief flooded through me. The old man had never made it to Lexington, never had to face the cold reality awaiting him there. His last Christmas Eve had ended on a hopeful note.

Nobody should feel unwanted on Christmas Eve.

32

The Father, the Son, and the Cosmic Spirit

Sheriff's departments in Tennessee are required by law to transport the mentally ill on emergency committals to psychiatric hospitals. This brings officers in contact with people who range from merely eccentric to what used to be called raving lunatics—in less enlightened times, of course. A few of them will always linger in an officer's mind.

One night while working as a jailer, I came in to work after a long weekend. As I went to the office to hang up my coat, I heard a voice singing loudly and fervently, "Amazing grace, how sweet the sound, that saved a wretch like me. I once was lost, but now I'm found. . . ." The voice was coming from a room that we called "The Barber Shop." During the day inmates could get their hair clipped by a trustee, and at night we used it for prisoners who needed to be watched closely. It was next to the office.

"What do we have in the barber shop?" I asked the sergeant.

"He burned down a house last Friday. Told the firemen that God ordered him to do it. He's been going on like that since we got him."

"Why isn't he in the hospital?" Even under Tennessee's mental health laws, arson qualifies as dangerous behavior.

"Who knows? We had him in the looney bin, but he was too violent." The looney bin was the popular name for the cell block where we kept mentally ill patients who had been refused admission to psychiatric hospitals because they were merely insane, not homicidal or suicidal. As much as possible, we kept them in one cell block.

I went to the back and relieved the afternoon shift. Two hours later the captain called me. "Come up here, and take off all your brass and jewelry. We're going to have to go in and truss up the crazy man."

"Here's the situation," the captain said. "He has somehow gotten the plastic panel out of the ceiling light."

"Captain, it's not humanly possible for anyone to jump that high," one of the other officers said.

"That's what we thought, but he's pulled it off. We have to get that plastic away from him before he hurts himself. This man is tremendously strong, so let's be careful."

We could hear the man's booming voice as we approached the steel door. "Open in the name of Jesus! I command you, door, open!"

"Hunter," the officer beside me said, "if that door opens, I'm gonna get the hell out of here."

The captain pushed the big brass key in the lock. It was immediately pushed back out by a sliver of plastic from the other side. This went on for several minutes, until the captain finally turned it before it could be pushed back.

"Let's do it," the captain said, throwing his weight against the door. Six of us pushed our way in. In doing so, someone fell against the light switch, enveloping us in almost total darkness. The air was filled with grunting and the breaking of plastic.

"He's beating me with the light guard," the captain yelled. "Hey, now somebody's punching me in the back. Stop it!"

Backing up, I felt along the wall until I found the light switch. I flipped it on and had my first glimpse of the insane man. I have fought prisoners who were on PCP and every other type of known hallucinogen. I have faced knives, guns, and clubs without panic. That night I almost broke and ran away.

He was about six feet tall, stringy, muscular, and totally naked. His frizzy brown hair stood around his head in a halo. The eyes were as red as those of a mongoose I once saw in *National Geographic*. The lips were drawn back in a snarl, and he was foaming at the mouth. He came directly toward me, eyes fixed on my face.

"Don't hurt him!" the captain yelled. To this day I do not know if the captain meant that I was not to hurt the prisoner or if he was telling him not to hurt me. I was alone on one side of the room. Everyone else was behind the prisoner.

Lazarus at the tomb looked like that prisoner. His name was Legion! These thoughts passed through my mind in the brief instant it took him to cross the room. The urge to run passed, and I threw a right hook that jarred my arm to the shoulder. The others took him from behind. We held him and poured tranquilizer down his throat.

Later, I sat on the bench in the booking area. Another officer came in and sat down by me. "Pretty weird," he said.

"Reminds me of *The Exorcist*," I replied.

"Yeah, if his head turns all the way around, we'd better call for a priest."

"His eyes reminded me of something," I said. "When I was driving an ambulance, we got a call to go to an old house in the country. Relatives thought something might be wrong.

"You could smell it as soon as we walked up on the porch. Somebody had been dead for a while. This old lady answered the door, just as if nothing was wrong. Her eyes had the same look as the guy in there. The woman had gone somewhere else. She had a vacant spot where her humanity used to be.

"She asked if we were there to check on John. We told her we were, and she said he had complained with chest pains for awhile but hadn't said anything about it in a couple of weeks.

"John had been dead for a couple of weeks. The mattress was soaked with body fluids. She had been *sleeping* with him. She was beyond odors and other such mundane affairs. Her humanity had just gone away, like the guy in the room back there. Where does a human soul go when it's not where it belongs?"

"What *is* human?" the other officer asked. "People rape and murder children, and we still call them human. He's just another screwed-up individual."

I knew he was right, but it took me a while to quit shivering every time I thought of the apparition coming at me in that little room. They finally shipped him off to a psychiatric ward, but his memory lingers.

On a warm, sunny afternoon, I was breaking in a rookie officer by the name of Bill Cowden. Like me, Bill got a late start in police work. He was past forty when he got through the academy and had the makings of a good officer. He was the kind of man you are glad to be training.

About 3:00 P.M. we were dispatched to check a car that had been abandoned on a freeway. The car was not stolen, so we had it towed in as a traffic hazard. We could not arrive at a logical explanation as to why it had been abandoned where we found it. As we were clearing, the dispatcher sent us to a shopping center to check on a disoriented subject who was wandering around the lot.

We found him, a frail little man graying and pale. "Hold it right there, friend. We need to talk to you a minute," I said. He tensed, as if preparing to run, but waited.

"Are you lost?" I asked.

"No. I had to leave my car and walk, but I'm not lost."

"What kind of car did you leave?" I asked.

"A 1972 Chevrolet, blue." I glanced at Cowden. It was the abandoned vehicle from the freeway.

"What was wrong with the car?" I asked.

"Nothing, I just had to leave it."

"*Why* did you have to leave it?" I pressed.

"Because the spirits told me to," he said, reluctantly.

"What spirits would that be?"

"Since 1979 I've been inhabited by the spirits of the Father, the Son, and the Cosmic Spirit," he said calmly.

"Let's step over to the car," I said with a smile. "There's something we need to check."

"I haven't done anything wrong," he answered.

"We know that," Cowden told him as he patted him down and put him in the cruiser.

A check with records confirmed what I expected. A mental health warrant was on file ordering any law enforcement officer to transport the man to the nearest hospital emergency room for evaluation.

"All right, friend," I said, "step out of the car. We have to put cuffs on you and take you to the hospital. Don't be alarmed. It's departmental policy."

"Officer, I have to warn you. In 1980 handcuffs were put on me, and it caused meteor showers and mass suicides all over the world. I can't control the spirits when they're upset."

"We'll have to take our chances," I told him, "because I have no choice. I do appreciate the warning, though."

At the hospital the emergency room doctor spent only a few minutes with him. He nodded for me to follow him into the hallway.

"Officer, did you really need my opinion on this one?"

"You're from out of state, aren't you, Doctor? I'd guess you've never tried to get an emergency committal in Tennessee."

"I can promise there'll be no problem with this one," he said, taking off his glasses to clean the lenses.

"I'll go get a cup of coffee while you're talking to the admitting physician at the psychiatric hospital."

When I returned, the young emergency room doctor was on the telephone and was red in the face. "Doctor, this man thinks he is inhabited by spirits. He's totally irrational.

"No, he has not threatened suicide. No, he has not assaulted or threatened assault, but he is not competent to care for himself. Well thanks one hell of a lot, Doctor!"

"Well?" I said, sipping my coffee.

"The admitting physician at the state hospital says they don't take crazy people," he answered. "I find this totally absurd."

"If *you* think it's absurd, talk to the families who have to live with insane people because of Tennessee law."

"So what are you going to do?"

"Whatever you say, Doctor. I did my part. You are now behind the eight-ball. What you generally do is write a short statement that you recommended hospitalization and were refused. That gives me permission to take him where I got him, or another place of his choice. If he goes berserk tonight and kills a dozen people, both of us are in the clear."

"Take the cuffs off, Bill," I said a few minutes later, doctor's letter in hand.

"You're turning me loose?" the little man asked in disbelief.

"Yep. You can walk out, or I'll take you back where I found you, or you can pick another place—inside the county, of course. Hopefully, we got the cuffs off before there is too much damage on a global scale."

"I'm sure the spirits will take how well you've treated me into consideration," the little man said. "Can you take me home—to my earthly home, I mean? I'm a little hungry."

A few minutes later we dropped him in front of his house. His elderly parents watched in horror as we let him out of the cruiser. I can imagine how it must be, living with the Father, the Son, and the Cosmic Spirit. The great state had spoken, however. 'Tis not ours to reason why.

"I almost broke out laughing a while ago," Cowden said.

"Why?"

"You were talking to him like the Father, the Son, and the Cosmic Spirit were real. You almost had me convinced that *you* were serious."

"He believed it, and we didn't have to fight with him. Besides, how do we know there weren't meteor showers and mass suicides when we cuffed him? If it turns out to be real, it can't hurt to have a friend on speaking terms with the Cosmic Spirit. Don't you agree?"

"I guess you're right," he chuckled. I noticed that for the rest of the shift he kept watching me out of the corner of his eye, as if trying to decide if I was really joking.

Epilogue

I t was, I think, Faith Baldwin who said something to the effect that nothing worthwhile emerges until a writer begins the "second million words." If this is the case, I have served my apprenticeship.

My point of view, I believe, is rare. I am a cop, and I write about cops. My experiences as an officer have been no more exciting than those of any hard-working cop. The difference? I was prepared to write about them.

When I began to write *The Moon Is Always Full*, I had no idea that so many people would eventually be touched by it. I saw it as a group of stories of interest to police officers nationwide and perhaps to a few interested individuals locally. I have been overwhelmed and overjoyed by the public response.

When I typed the last line, it was with the feeling that I had exhausted the subject. However, once my brother and sister officers began to hear of what I had done, I was deluged with calls.

"Did you tell the story about this or that?" they would ask. "Surely you didn't leave out the one about . . . ."

Soon I was at work again. There are so many stories that cry out to be told; the second book is now well under way.

Science fiction writers have long toyed with the idea of including a poet on future space voyages. I believe that is a marvelous idea. No matter how precise or how well-written, a technical report cannot express the majesty of mother earth hanging in the black void of space.

Only a gifted poet can do that.

It is the job of a poet to describe and define the universe, whether that of outer or inner space, or of a domestic disturbance call in an obscure county in the state of Tennessee.

In this modern age of specialization, poets tend to congregate in classrooms, far removed from the real world. This was not always so; there was a time when the bard went to war. With no newspapers or electronic journalism, who else would tell the story?

I have avoided the classroom all my life. This is not because classrooms are useless—they are not—but because what I wanted was not be found in academia.

I was a poet in search of a saga.

Among the boisterous, tough, and sometimes profane men and women of the world of law enforcement, I found my tongue and my song. Here is life at its most elemental, stripped of all triviality. Thoreau went to Walden Pond seeking life in its simplest form. I found it on the streets of Knox County, Tennessee.

I am not so arrogant as to think that I can speak for all cops. We are a diverse lot. However, I have been there, and when I speak of sweating palms and knees knocking together in terror, cops know I am telling the truth. I have not been a general, directing the battle from the rear, but a "grunt," down in the mud and the gravel with the warriors.

Few people find the satisfaction that has been mine. I am a man most blessed, a poet with a song. I have been able to share the heritage of those who put their bodies between society and chaos.

The Moon Is Always Full is not my story alone, but that of a group which generally has had to depend on outsiders to speak for them. I am one of them, and it is for them that I write, humbly.

And the story continues. . . .

Glossary of Commonly Used Police Codes

All professions produce a codified language. I endeavored to explain each code as I went along, but from time to time I let one slip by without explanation. I apologize for the confusion.

10 Codes

10-4 "I heard" or "I acknowledge."
10-22 "Disregard last traffic" or "Cancel call."
10-25 "I have made contact with" or "I have stopped. . ."
10-45 "Auto accident, no injury."
10-46 "Auto accident, with injury."
10-58 "Intoxicated person."
10-59 "Fight."
10-83 "Domestic problem."
10-85 "Fight."
10-96 "Check property." Loosely, "take a look at."

Officer Response Codes

Code A "Report made."
Code J Technically, "Property checks O.K." Loosely, "Everything is all right here. No problem."
Code O "Officer needs help, quickly!"